W9-BFR-790

CONTENTS

This book is a complete bridge course, taking the beginner to intermediate caliber. The player who knows the rules and has some experience can skip Day 1 but should not skip Day 2, since this introduces the Asset method of valuation, used throughout.

This book was originally published in 1985 as *Basic Bridge in 3 Weeks*. The new edition has been revised to reflect changes in bidding practice since that time, especially in the area of notrump bidding ranges and the use of transfer bids.

The bidding style is the modern one that is standard in clubs and tournaments. The chief differences between this and the traditional style used in social games are set out on page 205. A glossary of unfamiliar terms is included at the back of the book.

I am most grateful to Dorothy Hayden Truscott for setting aside her own writing in order to help me complete this book.

BRIDGE IN

3

WEEKS

YOUR FIRST DEAL

Here you are, sitting at a card table with three other bridge players. The one opposite you is your partner. Somebody deals the cards clockwise, one at a time, so that everyone has thirteen. You take a look at yours, being careful that nobody else can see them.

Sort your cards into suits, and sort each suit: the ace ranks high, then king, queen, jack, ten, and so on down to the two. When you have done this your hand turns out to be this:

♠ A K 8 7 6 3   ♡ 5 4 2   ◊ J 6   ♣ J 5

In each suit the highest card is shown on the left, which is the way most players prefer. In bridge the suits also have a rank, as shown. Starting at the bottom with clubs, they are in alphabetical order. Highest of all is notrump, which will be explained shortly[1]. This order is very important, as we shall see later, so memorize it:

Notrump
Spades
Hearts
Diamonds
Clubs

The first phase of each deal is the **bidding**, or auction. This determines the vital guidelines for the **play**, which is the second phase.

In this chapter we are concerned with *what* happens, rather than with *why*. Your partner dealt the cards, so he is entitled to start the action. He could say 'Pass' to indicate he does not wish to be involved for the time being. Instead he announces, 'One notrump'.

---

1. Strictly speaking, of course, 'notrump' is not a suit, but we can avoid a great deal of linguistic complication by referring to it as one.

This is a bid that starts the auction. It will be exactly like a commercial auction: every bid must be higher than the one before, and the highest bid wins. Since partner is the first player not to say 'Pass' at his turn to bid, he is said to have **opened the bidding**.

A bid in 'Notrump' suggests that the eventual play be carried out without **any trump suit**. The significance of having a trump suit will become clear shortly.

Every bid consists of a number followed by a suit, or perhaps, as in this case, by notrump.

The number you bid is the number of tricks *over six* that you are offering to take in the play. (A **trick** consists of four cards, one from each player.) Each of your thirteen cards will eventually be played, one at a time, so there will be thirteen tricks. The highest possible bid is therefore seven, an offer to take all the tricks (six plus seven equals thirteen).

Your partner's bid of one notrump therefore suggests that the partnership hands in combination take seven tricks without a trump suit. But that will be the final bid only if the next three players all say 'Pass', and that is not very likely.

The auction goes clockwise around the table, so before you can bid it is the turn of the player on your right. If he wants to bid he must go higher than one notrump, but he chooses to say 'Pass'.

Bidding more than the minimum number is often desirable and you should do it now. You could bid 'Two spades', but firmly and clearly you announce, 'Four spades'.

This is an offer for the partnership to take ten tricks (six plus four) with spades as the trump suit.

The reason for this apparently extravagant 'jump' bid is connected with the scoring. (For details, see the next chapter and page 218.)

For now, it is enough to note that the following contracts are very desirable:

Three notrump (nine tricks)
Four hearts (ten tricks)
Four spades (ten tricks)

We therefore jump to the desirable four-spade contract, expecting to make ten tricks.

It happens that our left-hand opponent thinks we have made a mistake. He says, 'Double'.

This approximately doubles the number of points at stake. Our partner and the other opponent both say 'Pass'.

If we felt very greedy we could say 'Redouble', again doubling the stakes. But we say 'Pass' and the bidding ends. Except at the start of the auction, three passes end the bidding because everyone has declined to bid higher.

Bid ends (handwritten annotation)

It is usual in bridge literature to name the four players by the compass points. If we call you South, your partner North, your left-hand opponent West, and your right-hand opponent East, the table will look like this:

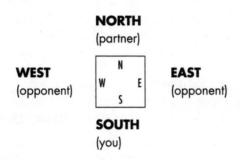

NORTH
(partner)

WEST
(opponent)

N
W   E
S

EAST
(opponent)

SOUTH
(you)

Now we can tabulate the bidding:

West	North	East	South
	One notrump	Pass	Four spades
Double	Pass	Pass	Pass

However, this can be abbreviated (and in future will be) like this:

West	North	East	South
	1NT	pass	4♠
dbl	all pass		

Notice that in these bidding diagrams, West's bids will always be in the far left column, no matter who deals or which player makes the first bid.

We have now struggled through the bidding of our first bridge deal. The first phase is over, and we must now play the hand. Remember that the contract is four spades doubled. Playing the North and South hands in combination, we must make at least ten

GAME (play starts) (handwritten annotation)

tricks out of the possible thirteen. Our opponents can frustrate us if they can make four or more.

We bid spades for the partnership, so we have to do all the work as **declarer**. Partner is the **dummy** and has nothing to do but sit back and admire our skillful play.

When you are the declarer the **opening lead** (the very first card played to the deal) always comes from your left-hand opponent. In this case, he produces the king of hearts and your partner puts down his hand on the other side of the table like this:

```
♠  ♡  ◊  ♣
9  A  A  A
2  8  K  7
   6  Q  4
      3  2
```

He will always put the trumps on his right, your left.

In future, however, we will show the suits horizontally, making them rather easier to read. The whole picture you see is therefore this:

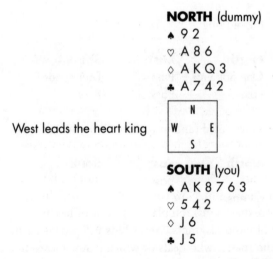

NORTH (dummy)
♠ 9 2
♡ A 8 6
◊ A K Q 3
♣ A 7 4 2

West leads the heart king

```
    N
W       E
    S
```

SOUTH (you)
♠ A K 8 7 6 3
♡ 5 4 2
◊ J 6
♣ J 5

Remember that our contract is four spades doubled: we are trying to take ten tricks out of a possible thirteen. A trick is a group of four cards, one from each of the four hands. These cards are played in clockwise sequence.

We now reach a vital matter: the significance of the trump suit.

The first card played (or led) to a trick sets a pattern: the other players must play the same suit if they are able to do so. In general the highest card played in that suit wins the trick, and the player who wins it has the right and duty to lead (play the first card) on the next trick.

However, a player who does not have any cards of the suit led can play anything he pleases. If his choice is a trump he will win the trick unless someone else plays a higher trump.

This may sound tricky, which is surely the right word. But it is easy when you try it and we shall now try it. You will probably find it helpful to take a deck of cards and carry out the following moves physically. Do not worry about why anything happens — for now, just study the procedure. *start Here (pg 8 - has diagram)*

Your plan is to win the first trick, so you pull dummy's ace of hearts into the middle of the table. East plays a small heart and you do the same from your hand.

You won this trick in dummy, so you must play from dummy. You choose the spade two — a trump. East plays a low spade, you play the ace and West plays a low spade.

Now you play the spade king, which is sure to win the trick. West plays the ten, you play the nine from dummy and East thinks a little. He does not have any spades and can therefore play any suit he pleases. He chooses a small club. When you fail to follow suit like this you are making a *discard*, a play that can never win a trick.

Next you play the jack of diamonds, which wins. The other hands play low diamonds. Next comes the six of diamonds from you and the queen from dummy, winning the trick. The opponents both play a low diamond.

Now you play the king of diamonds from the dummy and your right-hand opponent follows suit. Now you have a chance to discard, since you have no more diamonds. You play your four of hearts.

As it happens West has no more diamonds either. He could discard a heart or a club, allowing dummy's king to win, but he chooses to play the spade jack. That wins the trick. Remember, a trump always wins a trick unless a higher trump is played. *X*

West has won the trick, so it is his turn to lead. He plays the heart queen, which wins the trick since the other hands play low hearts. But when he continues with the jack of hearts, collecting small hearts from dummy and his partner, it is your turn to trump. You have no more hearts, so you play the three of spades, a trump that wins the trick.

You would like the lead to be in the dummy, so you play the five of clubs. West plays the ten, you play the ace from dummy and East follows with a low club. Now you play the ace of diamonds, and again discard, this time the club jack.

West can trump, or **ruff** (which means the same thing). He wins the trick by playing the spade queen. But you make the last three tricks because you have the only remaining trumps.

You have made the ten tricks you contracted for in the bidding and scored a **game**, which is worth bonus points. Your left-hand opponent is sorry he doubled. How the scoring works in detail is not important at this stage. It is described on page 218.

If you are quite sure you understand this, go straight on to the lesson for Day 2. If you do not feel confident, study the following diagrams of the deal, bidding, and play. Then try the quiz.

NORTH (dummy)
♠ 9 2
♡ A 8 6
◇ A K Q 3
♣ A 7 4 2

WEST
♠ Q J 10 4
♡ K Q J 9
◇ 8 4
♣ K Q 10

EAST
♠ 5
♡ 10 7 3
◇ 10 9 7 5 2
♣ 9 8 6 3

K Deal

SOUTH
♠ A K 8 7 6 3
♡ 5 4 2
◇ J 6
♣ J 5

West	North	East	South
	1NT	pass	4♠
dbl	all pass		

Bidding

Below is a diagram of the play. (The card in boldface type wins the trick.)

play

Trick	West	North	East	South
1	♡ K	♡ **A**	♡ 3	♡ 2
2	♠ 4	♠ 2	♠ 5	♠ **A**
3	♠ 10	♠ 9	♣ 3	♠ **K**
4	♢ 4	♢ 3	♢ 2	♢ **J**
5	♢ 8	♢ **Q**	♢ 5	♢ 6
6	♠ **J**	♢ K	♢ 7	♡ 4
7	♡ **Q**	♡ 6	♡ 7	♡ 5
8	♡ J	♡ 8	♡ 10	♠ **3**
9	♣ 10	♣ **A**	♣ 6	♣ 5
10	♠ **Q**	♢ A	♢ 9	♣ J
11				♠ **6**
12				♠ **7**
13				♠ **8**

(*Note:* When, near the end of the play, it is quite obvious what the result will be, a player may show his cards and **claim**. Here South would claim by showing his three trumps after ten tricks had been played. This saves time.)

QUIZ

1. Which of the red suits is higher in rank?

2. Which are the most desirable contracts?

3. If the player on your right bids three diamonds, what is the cheapest call you can make (a) in spades? (b) in clubs?

4. How does the bidding end?

5. Who becomes the dummy?

6. Who makes the opening lead?

7. Who makes subsequent leads?

8. How do you win a trick?

QUIZ ANSWERS

1. Hearts outrank diamonds. Remember, the suits are in alphabetical order starting at the bottom, with notrump on top of the heap:

   Notrump
   Spades
   Hearts
   Diamonds
   Clubs

2. Three notrump, four spades, and four hearts. These score a game, which is worth extra points, directly or indirectly. All contracts higher than four spades also score a game, but they are rarer and harder.

3. (a) Three spades. Spades are higher than diamonds, so they can be bid at the same level.
   (b) Four clubs. Clubs rank below diamonds, so we must go to a higher level.

4. The bidding almost always ends with three consecutive passes. The exception is the beginning of the bidding: if the first three players pass, the fourth man must have his chance. If he also passes we have a **pass-out** or **throw-in**: there is no play at all and we redeal.

5. The declarer's partner is the dummy. Often, but by no means always, the player who makes the final bid is the declarer. This is not true when a bid is **supported** (i.e. both partners at some stage bid the same suit) and the final contract is in that suit. In that case, the player who had the original idea is the declarer: for example, if I bid one notrump and my partner bids three notrump I am the declarer and he is the dummy.

6. The player on declarer's left.

7. The player who won the previous trick.

8. By playing any trump, or the highest trump if there is more than one in the trick. Otherwise, by playing the highest card of the suit led.

ESSENTIALS TO REMEMBER

1. The ranking order is: clubs (low); diamonds; hearts; spades; notrump (high).

2. A trick is four cards played in clockwise order. The first card requires the other players to play the same suit, and the highest card wins. Exception: a player who has no cards in that suit can discard another suit, or win the trick by playing a trump. If there is more than one trump, high wins.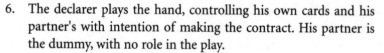

3. The player who wins the trick starts the next trick. There are 13 tricks altogether.

4. A bid indicates the number of tricks above six you propose to make.

5. Desirable contracts are: three notrump (nine tricks); four hearts or four spades (ten tricks).

6. The declarer plays the hand, controlling his own cards and his partner's with intention of making the contract. His partner is the dummy, with no role in the play.

(handwritten) 3NT = 9 pts
4H = 10 pts
4S = 10 pts ←

If you are going to attempt one of the three desirable game contracts you will need much more than your share of the high cards, roughly two-thirds, to have a fair chance of succeeding. A long suit would also be a help.

Common sense suggests that the more aces, kings, and queens you have the better. Some way of measuring the strength of a hand is needed, and we use a **point-count**.

Ace counts	4 points
King counts	3 points
Queen counts	2 points
Jack counts	1 point
total in each suit	**10 points**

(handwritten: HCP — High Card Points)

Now you can add something for a long suit if you have one. If you have any suit with five cards or more, count an extra point. With two long suits count a point for each.

We said that you need about two-thirds of the high-card strength to attempt a game. Two-thirds of 40 (the total in the deck) is 26 and change. Ignore the change, and we have a vital number: *bid game with 26 points.*

That means, of course, 26 points in the combined partnership hands. With fewer, you normally stop short of game.

At the start you know your points, but what your partner has is a mystery. The bidding solves the mystery. Suppose your partner bids one notrump. ↴

In standard bridge this is a very accurate bid, which tells you two things: he has exactly 15, 16, or 17 points, and his hand is **balanced**, which means that he has no very long suit (a suit longer than five cards), no very short suit (a suit with fewer than two cards), and no more than one **doubleton** (a two-card suit). *and no voids*

It is now rather easy to decide whether the partnership hands justify a game bid of three notrump. Suppose your hand is:

♠ 4 2   ♡ J 6 4   ◇ Q 4 3   ♣ A Q 10 7 6

How many points do you have? It may look like 9, but if you remember to add 1 point for the long suit the answer is 10.

Should you bid a game?

Probably. You have 10 points and your partner has at least 15. More often than not, the total will be 26, the vital number.

What do you bid?

Three notrump. When you know what the contract should be, go right ahead and bid it. Neither of the other normal game contracts, four hearts and four spades, has any appeal. Do not worry about your weakness in spades. Particular suits are not important, whether you are opening the bidding or responding to partner's opening. What matters is your overall distribution and total strength.

Your bid announces that you expect to have 26 points in the combined hands and that notrump is right.

What will your partner do? Pass, of course, without thinking. He has described his hand accurately, and you have made a final decision for the partnership.

Now suppose that your hand is weaker.

♠ K 4 2   ♡ 5 2   ◇ Q J 8 6   ♣ J 9 5 4

How many points do you have?

You have 7.

Are there prospects of game?

No. Your partner has at most 17, and you have 7. The total cannot be 26.

So what do you do?

Pass. That is usually right when game is out of reach. Your contract is called a **partscore**, which simply means 'less than game'. This has some value, and it is obviously better to have a small plus score, for making a contract, than a minus score for bidding an unsuccessful game.

Now try this one. You have almost the same hand. Again, your partner has started the bidding with one notrump.

♠ K J 2   ♡ 5 2   ◊ Q J 8 6 3   ♣ J 9 5

How many points do you have?

You have 9: 8 in high cards and 1 for the long diamond suit.

Is game certain? Possible? Or impossible?

Possible. Partner might have 17 points, which would give you the necessary 26-point total.

What do you bid?

Two notrump, announcing hope of game and therefore promising 8 or 9 points. Partner will pass with 15 and go on with 16 or 17. (Yes, if he has 16 we'll be 1 point short of our requirement. We cannot be right on target every time. 'Most of the time' is good enough.)

Now we get to a new and exciting word: **slam**.

Everyone (or almost everyone) has heard of a grand slam in baseball: a mighty blow that scores the maximum.

Baseball borrowed the term from bridge. If you can bid to seven successfully, which means making all thirteen tricks, you have a **grand slam**. You collect a very big bonus — perhaps we should say a grand bonus.

This is very rare, but very gratifying when it happens. Much more common is a bid of six, a try for a **small slam**. As you would expect, when this succeeds it is worth a small bonus — smaller than the grand slam bonus, but well worth having.

Here again there are some vital numbers: 33 points justifies a small slam effort, and 37 points a grand slam.

This gives us four bidding zones. In tabular form:

Partnership Points	Zone	Tricks Needed
Fewer than 26	Partscore	Usually 7 or 8
26-32	Game	Usually 9 or 10
33-36	Small slam	12
37-40	Grand slam	13

Now it is time for you to bid and play a hand. Your partner deals and bids one notrump. The opponents pass whenever it is their turn. You must decide what to bid with this hand.

♠ Q 4   ♡ K Q 6 3   ◇ A K 9 5 2   ♣ Q J

The first thing you note is that you do not have a very short suit, which would make notrump unpalatable. So the only question you have to worry about is: how many notrump?

Answer these questions:

1. How many points do you have?

2. How many points does your partner have?

3. What zone do you belong in?

4. What do you bid?

5. What do you expect your partner to do next?

6. Who is the dummy?

7. Who makes the opening lead?

No doubt you found the questions easy and arrived at these answers:

1. You have 18 points, counting 1 point for the long diamond suit. The quick way to count this hand is to start with the minor suits, clubs and diamonds: an ace-king-queen-jack group is 10 points. Then add in the major suits, spades and hearts, and the point for the long suit.

2. He has 15-17.

3. Small slam: $18 + 15 = 33$. There is no chance of the 37 needed for a grand slam even if your partner has 18.

4. Six notrump. When you know the right contract, go ahead and bid it. When your partner bids one notrump (or any other descriptive bid) you are the Captain of the Partner Ship and make all the major decisions.

5. Partner will pass automatically. You have made the decision — his not to reason why.

6. You are the dummy. Notrump was originally your partner's idea, and all you did was support him.

7. Your right-hand opponent. He puts the jack of hearts face upward on the table to start the ball rolling. You put your thirteen cards face upward on the table so that they are all clearly visible.

In real life you would now relax as dummy while your partner battled away to make twelve tricks with the combined hands. But you would not learn much that way so we shall break the rules. Let us suppose that your partner is called to the telephone. With the opponents' permission, you move around the table into your partner's seat and become the declarer. This is what you see:

DUMMY

♠ Q 4
♡ K Q 6 3
◊ A K 9 5 2
♣ Q J

West leads the heart jack

	N	
W		E
	S	

DECLARER

♠ K J 6
♡ A 5 2
◊ 4 3
♣ A K 8 7 5

It is your turn to play from the dummy, and you may already be reaching for a card. If so, you are committing a common bridge folly.

When the play starts you must take a minute or two to study the two hands in combination and form a plan. Experts do that and so should you. Let the opponents wait. It will please your partner to know that you are trying hard and not playing random cards thoughtlessly.

The basic thing to remember, of course, is how many tricks you are aiming to make (in this case twelve). And how many tricks you can afford to lose (in this case one).

What trick do you expect to lose?

Obviously the ace of spades. So you cannot afford to lose any tricks in the other suits.

To find the twelve needed tricks you must look at each suit in turn.

You look for *fast* tricks and *slow* tricks. Fast tricks can be taken without losing the lead and should usually be kept in reserve. Slow tricks cannot be taken without losing the lead, and should usually be developed quickly.

Fast tricks and slow tricks can be classified under three headings: *sure*, *probable*, and *possible*.

With this in mind, look at each suit in turn, starting with spades. What sort of tricks are available? Are there any pitfalls? Make your assessment before reading on.

Ready?

In spades you can see:

Q 4

K J 6

The opponents' ace will capture one of your three honor cards and the other two will take tricks. In general, *their tricks plus your tricks equals length of suit.*

You have two slow tricks, and you will want to play this suit at an early stage. *Slow* tricks need *quick* work.

In hearts you can see:

K Q 6 3

A 5 2

The ace-king-queen represent three 'fast sure' tricks. There is no hurry for these, although one of them will have to be played right away since West has led a heart.

There is also a 'fast possible' trick here. If you are lucky each of the opponents will have exactly three hearts. Then the heart six in dummy will take a trick after the ace, king, and queen have been played. In diamonds you can see:

A K 9 5 2

4 3

The ace and king are two 'fast sure' tricks, which will be kept in reserve. Fast tricks are played slowly.

There are also one or two 'slow possible' tricks, but they are of no interest because you cannot afford to lose a diamond trick to develop them.

In clubs you can see:

Q J

A K 8 7 5

The ace, king, queen, and jack represent four 'fast sure' tricks. By the time these have been played it is highly likely that the opponents' clubs will have been exhausted. So the eight of clubs in your hand is a 'fast probable' trick. The only danger is that one opponent has five or six of the missing clubs.

Scoring the club tricks is not so easy, however. There is a road-block lurking, or **block** for short.

It is important to be in the right hand at the right time. To solve all block problems there is a simple rule: *play high from short*.

In this case dummy is short in clubs, so we must start by playing dummy's high clubs, the queen and jack. This makes it easy to play the remaining clubs when the lead is in your hand. For that you will need an **entry**, or way of gaining the lead in the appropriate hand, in another suit. The obvious entry is the ace of hearts, so be careful not to play that card too quickly.

It is time to sum up your prospects. Answer two questions:

1. Can you count twelve probable tricks?

2. Where do you plan to win the first trick?

Your answers should be:

1. Yes. Eleven sure (two spades, three hearts, two diamonds, and four clubs) and one very probable club trick.

2. In dummy with the heart queen (or the king). You must save the ace in your hand as an entry.

As you have a complete assessment, the actual play will be easy. Two more questions:

1. Which suit will you play first?

2. Which suit will you play second, and how many times will you lead it?

Your answers should be:

1. Clubs. Play the queen and jack to unblock. Watch to see if both opponents follow suit. If they do, your 'fast probable' trick, the club eight, becomes a 'fast sure' trick and the slam is sure to succeed. If they don't, you can still hope for the 'fast possible' trick in hearts.

2. Spades. Play the queen, following the 'high from short' rule. If the queen wins play one more round, but no more.

The rest is plain sailing. Assuming the clubs break evenly, you will find that you have made five club tricks, three heart tricks, two spade tricks, and two diamond tricks, for a total of twelve.

You have made your first slam. Congratulations!

QUIZ

1. If your hand is exactly average in high cards, with no long suit, how many points do you have?

2. Counting high cards only, what is the theoretical maximum for a single thirteen-card hand?

3. If your partner bids one notrump and you raise to six notrump holding 18 high-card points, could the opponents have two aces?

4. If you have a balanced hand with 16 points, what should you bid if your partner opens one notrump?

5. What do you respond to a one notrump opening if you have a balanced hand with 22 points?

6. If you have a balanced hand and partner opens one notrump, what notrump bids by you give him options?

7. How would you play the suit below?

    ♠ A J 3 2
    ♠ K Q 4

8. How many tricks would you hope to make in the suit below?

    ◇ Q J 10 9 8 7
    ◇ 3 2

QUIZ ANSWERS

1. You have 10 points (ace + king + queen + jack = 4 + 3 + 2 + 1 = 10).
   Or to put it another way: 40 (the total points in the deck) ÷ 4 = 10.

2. The maximum is 37 — all the aces, kings, and queens, plus one
   jack. The missing three jacks represent 3 points out of 40.

3. Possible, but once in a lifetime, so do not worry. Partner would
   have to have 14 high-card points and 1 long-suit point.

4. Four notrump. This is an invitation to six notrump, and partner will
   continue unless his hand is a minimum. Your bid shows that slam
   is possible but not certain. Your point-count must be 16 or 17.

5. Seven notrump (22 + 15 = 37).

6. Two notrump or four notrump, both of which ask him to continue
   unless his hand is a minimum. If you bid any other number of
   notrump he will pass automatically because you have made a
   final decision for the partnership.

7. Play the king and queen first, following the high-from-short rule.
   Then you will score the ace and jack without having to worry
   about an entry in another suit. If you start with the ace or jack you
   create an awkward block.

8. Four (assuming no tricks are trumped by your opponents). If you
   keep leading this suit you can force the opponents to take their
   ace and king. Their two tricks and your four tricks add up to six
   — the length of your suit.

ESSENTIALS TO REMEMBER

1. The deck has 40 points. An average hand has 10 points.

2. Bid to a game with 26 points, a small slam with 33 points, and a grand slam with 37 points.

3. A one notrump opening shows 15-17 points. Partner totals the points, searching for game or slam.

4. Make a plan when the dummy comes down, before playing any cards.

5. Assess each suit in terms of fast, slow, sure, probable, and possible tricks. Count your winners and their winners. (The total should be thirteen. If it is not, try to see why.)

6. Your tricks plus their tricks equals length of suit.

7. Play high cards from short hand first.

8. Go after the slow tricks early. There is no hurry for fast tricks.

So far we have been concerned with only notrump bidding and play. But now we must deal with suit contracts, which greatly outnumber notrump. The requirement for game is still 26 points.

The first important thing to note is that *length* is what counts in choosing a trump suit. The strength of a suit is of little consequence. And just as we worried in the last lesson, and will continue to worry, about combined point count — counting the two hands together — we have to worry about *combined length* in choosing a trump suit.

Obviously it would be foolish to choose a trump suit in which the opponents have the majority of the trumps. That would give them the advantage. And choosing a suit in which you have only a slender majority is not desirable either.

What you look for in the bidding is a suit in which the partnership has at least eight cards. And the more the merrier.

Combined Trumps	Verdict
6 or fewer	disastrous
7	bad
8	normal
9	good
10	excellent
11 or more	incredible

Maj
NT
Min

However, all suits are not equal. As we already know, game contracts in the **major suits** — four hearts and four spades — are desirable, assuming 26 combined points. To make game in clubs or diamonds, the **minor suits**, we have to bid five. This means making eleven tricks, and it is almost always better to try for nine tricks in three notrump.

Putting these two elements together we have a vital general rule: find a major with at least eight cards in the combined hands.

If you find the eight-card major fit, with 26 combined points, you know where to play a game. If you cannot find one, three notrump is almost sure to be right.

The search for the eight-card fit is very easy when your partner opens one notrump. Remember that you are the Captain, and make all the major decisions.

Look back for a moment to the first deal in this course, on page 8. The South hand has 10 points, counting 1 for his long suit. And he knows that the combined hands have at least eight spades.

How does he know that? Because he has six, and the notrump bid promised a balanced hand with at least two cards in each suit. With only one spade (a **singleton**), North would not have bid one notrump.

South therefore jumped to four spades knowing that the combined hands had enough strength and enough combined spade length. He made a final decision for the partnership.

A rather more common situation calling for a final decision occurs when you are weaker. Suppose partner opens one notrump and you have:

♠ J 9 5 3 2   ♡ 4   ◇ 6 5 2   ♣ 9 8 5 2

With such a hand there is an obvious temptation to say 'pass' without thinking. But that is an error. You should bid two *spades*[1].

It is very likely, though not certain, that you have at least eight spades in the combined hands. Two spades will probably go down a trick or two, but you must expect a minus score when your hand is very weak.

The point to realize is that while two spades will be a poor contract, one notrump will be even worse. It is likely that your hand will take no tricks at all. In spades your hand should be worth two or three tricks.

Two spades is a final decision for the partnership. It simply says: We have no chance of game, partner. And two spades is preferable to one notrump.

---

1. Once you are past the beginner stage, you will want to use a **transfer bid** here. You will bid two hearts, which will show spade length, with the intention of passing partner's required response of two spades. See page 152)

Your partner passes automatically. (If he bids you have the wrong partner and should trade him or her in at the earliest opportunity.)

Of course you would be happier if you held six spades, guaranteeing an eight-card fit, and happier too if you had a few more points. But you cannot have more than 8 points, because 9 would be enough to give the 26 needed for game if partner has a 17-point maximum notrump.

In other situations you will ask your partner a question. Suppose he opens one notrump and you have this:

♠ A Q J 10 3　　♡ 6 4 2　　◇ Q 3　　♣ J 10 3

You have 11 points, counting 1 for the long spade suit. You can count at least 26 in the combined hands, so you can head for game. Which game?

You are not sure. It is likely, but not certain, that partner has at least three spades and that you have a normal fit or better. But if he has only two spades the fit is bad and you would wish to play three notrump.

The bid you should make is *three spades* (but see page 152 when you are ready for more advanced methods).

This is called a **jump** bid (or sometimes a **skip** bid). Here you have jumped, or skipped, past two spades. When you skip exactly one level in a new suit in this fashion you guarantee game or slam. This is a **forcing** bid, demanding that partner continue at least to game. You promise that the combined strength is at least 26 points.

If your partner passes three spades he is a nincompoop and you can be mad at him — just as mad as if he failed to pass a bid of two spades.

Your bid of three spades promises five cards in spades (just possibly more) and asks this question: '*Do you have three (or more) spades?*'

In other words, your jump to three spades asks partner if he has spades with you – at least three of them, as you are trying to find the magic eight-card fit. (And a jump to three hearts would ask similarly whether partner has three or more hearts.) If your partner hates spades, because he has only a doubleton, he will back away by bidding three notrump. You will fold your tent, because you will know that the spade fit is bad.

If your partner has three spades, or more, he will **support** you by bidding four spades. You are sure of a normal eight-card fit or better. The bidding is now over. It went like this:

West	North	East	South
	1NT	pass	3♠
pass	4♠	all pass	

You are declarer as South because spades was originally your idea. West leads the jack of diamonds, and your partner puts down his hand as dummy. You have to make ten tricks with this layout:

NORTH
♠ 5 4 2
♡ K Q 7 5
◇ A K
♣ A 7 5 2

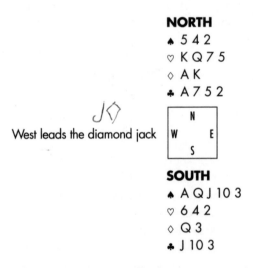

West leads the diamond jack

```
      N
  W       E
      S
```

SOUTH
♠ A Q J 10 3
♡ 6 4 2
◇ Q 3
♣ J 10 3

Again, as you work through the play of this hand, you will probably find it helpful to use a deck of cards and actually play each card as you come to it.

In planning the play you must bear in mind a basic principle: *lead from low cards toward high cards.*

This allows you to take advantage of a favorable position of the opponents' high cards.

Now do the usual survey of the combined hands, starting with spades. Make up your mind how many losers there are in each suit. If the answer is not clear, *consider sure losers and possible losers.*

low toward high

Ready?

In spades we have no sure losers, but we may lose a trick to the king. To avoid that, we try to insure that our ace captures the king at some stage.

If you could choose, which opponent would you prefer to have the king?

The answer is clearly East, on your right. He has to play *before* you, or *in front* of you (some would say *under* you).

If he has the king, you can save your ace until the king is played.

We often have to make assumptions, in bridge as in life, and here we *assume* that East has the king. If West has that card the chance that we can prevent him from taking a trick is negligible.

How will we attack the spades? Obviously by leading from the dummy, *low toward high*. The plan is to play a middle card from the hand unless East produces the king. This maneuver is a **finesse**, one of the basic maneuvers of bridge. It is an attempt to score an extra trick or two by assuming a favorable lie of the enemy cards.

In spades, therefore, we have no sure loser but one possible loser. We have a 50 percent chance of finding the spade king with East, and avoiding that loser.

Now look at hearts. The heart ace is a sure trick for the opponents, so we have one sure loser.

Which opponent would you prefer to have the ace?

West, on your left. If he has that card you can prevent him from using his ace to capture one of dummy's high cards.

How will you play? _Low toward high_, of course. If West has the ace and plays it, you can play low from dummy, preserving your high cards. And if he plays low dummy can win the trick.

If East has the ace, however, he will surely be able to capture the king or queen. You will take only one trick, and will lose two tricks.

So the heart suit has one sure loser and one possible loser.

The club suit is shaky, with two likely losers. You should leave the clubs alone.

How about diamonds?

Clearly there are no losers, for after two rounds have been played you can trump. How many diamond winners are there? Beware of a little trap. If your answer was 'three', you have had what bridge players call a 'blind spot'. This is the standard excuse for a stupid error in the play or defense.

It is true that you have the ace, king, and queen, but they are not worth three tricks. The queen is doomed to fall wastefully under one of dummy's high cards. You can never take three tricks in a suit unless you have at least three cards of that suit in one hand or the other.

To sum up, you have five possible losers: two in hearts, two in clubs and one in spades. If you can avoid two of these you will make your contract. The opponents will have three tricks, which is exactly the number you can afford to lose.

Now we have finished planning, let's play. The diamond lead offers no choice. We win with the king in the dummy, which is convenient. We would like to lead trumps from the dummy, low to high, and can do so right now.

When we lead a spade from the dummy East plays low. What do you play from your hand?

The queen, a finesse against East's assumed king. (The jack or ten are as good.) West plays the seven of spades, so he presumably does not have the king. Our finesse has succeeded. What next?

We would like to repeat the finesse. But the lead is in our hand since the queen won the trick. We could play a diamond, but it is slightly better to play a heart: low to high in that suit while we have a convenient opportunity.

We hope that West has the heart ace, but East turns out to have that card and uses it to capture dummy's queen. He returns a diamond to the ace in dummy.

Now we lead another spade. East plays low and we play the jack (or the ten) with confidence. As we expect, the repeat finesse succeeds.

West follows suit, and we do a little counting. We had a normal eight-card trump fit, so the opponents began with five trumps. We have seen four of them, so the king is the only one left. We play the trump ace, and as planned East has to play the king.

Now we lead to the heart king, and both opponents follow. The position you see is now this:

NORTH
♠ —
♡ 7 5
◇ —
♣ A 7 5 2

SOUTH
♠ 10 3
♡ 6
◇ —
♣ J 10 3

How many hearts are left in the opponents' hands? The easiest way to think about this is to count *their* cards, not yours. They began with six hearts out of thirteen (you had seven) and they have each followed twice. That leaves them with two, so you play another heart hoping that their hearts will appear together. They do, so your last heart in the dummy is **established**. It is the thirteenth and last heart in the deck, so it will score a trick when you play it.

Whatever the opponents do now, you have your ten tricks. When you eventually reach dummy with the club ace you will play your heart winner and throw a club loser. Your opponents take two heart tricks and one club trick.

The complete deal was this:

NORTH
♠ 5 4 2
♡ K Q 7 5
◇ A K
♣ A 7 5 2

WEST
♠ 7 6
♡ J 9 3
◇ J 10 9 6 2
♣ Q 9 8

```
    N
 W     E
    S
```

EAST
♠ K 9 8
♡ A 10 8
◇ 8 7 5 4
♣ K 6 4

SOUTH
♠ A Q J 10 3
♡ 6 4 2
◇ Q 3
♣ J 10 3

1. In choosing a trump suit, what is more important: length or strength?

2. How many combined trumps constitute a normal fit?

3. If you can count 26 points and plan to bid game, what do you look for?

4. If your partner opened one notrump, what would you respond with each of the following hands?

    a) ♠ 4   ♡ Q J 7 6 4   ◊ J 2   ♣ Q 10 9 3 2
    b) ♠ 4   ♡ 9 8 7 6 4 3   ◊ 3 2   ♣ A K Q 2
    c) ♠ 4   ♡ A K 7 6 4   ◊ 3 2   ♣ A K J 6 4

5. Suppose that you are playing three notrump and must play a suit with three small cards in your hand and some strength in the dummy. You plan, of course, to play low to high. Assess your prospects, on a best-case and worst-case basis, if dummy has:

    a) K 2
    b) A Q
    c) Q J 2
    d) K J 10
    e) A J 10

1. Length matters. Strength is relatively unimportant.

2. Eight cards is a normal fit. More, of course, would be even better.

3. Look for a major suit, spades or hearts, with at least eight cards in the combined hands. If you cannot find one, it is probably right to bid three notrump.

4. (a) Two hearts[2]. This is a final decision, and partner will pass. A normal fit is likely, and game is out of reach. You have 7 points, counting both long suits, and partner has at the most 17.

   (b) Four hearts. This is a final decision, and partner will pass. Since partner has guaranteed at least two hearts you know there is a normal fit or better. You can count 26 combined points, since you have 10 in high cards and 1 for the long suit.

   (c) Three hearts[3]. A question: do you have three or more hearts, partner? If partner bids four hearts, showing three- or four-card support, you have found a normal fit and will probably play six hearts. Counting a point for each long suit the combined hands must have at least the 33 points needed for a small slam. If your partner bids three notrump, showing that he has only two hearts, six clubs will be a plausible contract. If he has only two hearts he must have at least three clubs so there will be a normal fit there. Remember that major suits are preferred for game contracts but any suit with a normal fit will do for slam.

5. (a) Hope for the ace on your left. In that case your king will take a trick. If the ace is on your right the king is doomed and you will take no tricks in the suit.

   (b) Hope for the king on your left. That will allow you to finesse the queen successfully, scoring two tricks. If the king is on your right the queen is doomed and you will have to settle for one trick.

   (c) Hope that the player on your left has the ace or the king or both. If you lead low to the jack and it loses, try low to the queen later. You will score a trick unless both ace and king are on your right, which would be very unlucky.

   (d) Hope that the player on your left has the queen, allowing you to make two tricks. The position of the ace is unimportant. Lead

---

2. Using transfer bids, described on p. 152, bid two diamonds, intending to pass partner's two hearts response.

3. Using the transfer bids described on p. 152, you would bid two diamonds, promising hearts, and then bid clubs, intending to bid a slam.

to the ten. If it loses to the queen you will score one trick later. But if West has the queen you can lead to the jack later and score two tricks.

(e) Hope that the player on your left has the king, or the queen, or both. Lead to the ten, and if that loses lead to the jack later. You will take two tricks except in the unlucky situation in which both the king and the queen are on your right.

ESSENTIALS TO REMEMBER

1. Length counts. The location of your strength is of little importance.

2. Eight cards in a suit in the combined hands is a normal fit. More is better.

3. If you plan to bid game, look for a major suit (spades or hearts) with at least eight cards in the combined hands. Fall back on three notrump if you have to.

4. If partner opens one notrump, major-suit responses[4] mean:

Bid	Strength	Meaning	Partner's Action
2♡ or 2♠	1-7 points	This is better than 1NT	Pass (automatically)
3♡ or 3♠	10+ points	5-card suit looking for normal fit	3NT with doubleton, raise with 3+
4♡ or 4♠	10-14 points	6+ suit	Pass (automatically)

(Responses in minor suits will be discussed later — see page 151.)

5. Lead from *low* cards toward *high* cards.

6. If it will help you, assume that the enemy high cards are where you would like them to be.

---

4. Or use the transfer responses described on page 152.

Bidding at bridge consists largely of descriptive bids, usually called **limited** because they define the hand within close limits, and vague bids, which leave partner in the dark. The idea is that someone will make a limited bid sooner or later, allowing partner to make a final decision.

With the one notrump opening bids we have discussed so far, the limited bid came immediately and the final decision usually followed at once. But the great majority of the hands you pick up are unsuitable for a one notrump bid, either because they are not balanced or because they are not in the 15-17 point range.

The usual way to start the ball rolling is with a bid of one of a suit: *one club, one diamond, one heart,* or *one spade.*

Since we are now suggesting a suit contract, we can give some value to short suits as well as to long suits and high cards: for a singleton suit (one card) count 1 point; for a void suit (no cards) count 2 points.

These extra points, for long suits and short suits, are called **assets**. Like financial assets, they may, as we shall see later, change in value.

Calculate the value of each of the following six hands:

a) ♠ K Q 6 4 2
    ♡ 9 8 3
    ◊ Q 9
    ♣ A J 6

b) ♠ K Q 7 6 4 2
    ♡ —
    ◊ A 8 6
    ♣ J 10 9 3

c) ♠ 6 5 4 3 2
    ♡ A K 8 4 2
    ◊ 3
    ♣ K 10

d) ♠ 4 3
    ♡ A K Q J
    ◊ 5 4 3 2
    ♣ K 4 2

e) ♠ 5
    ♡ A 4 3 2
    ◊ A 4 3 2
    ♣ A 4 3 2

f) ♠ K Q 4 2
    ♡ 4 3 2
    ◊ A 4 2
    ♣ A 4 2

You should have arrived at the same answer for all six hands: 13 points.

If not, look again. You may have forgotten an asset for a long suit or a short suit.

Thirteen points is a vital number: it is the minimum needed to open the bidding with one of a suit.

There is logic to this: 13 is exactly half of the combined strength needed for game. If you and your partner each pass with 12 points, not much harm is done. But if you each pass with 13 you have missed a game — a bidding disaster.

So all the above hands just rate an opening bid of one of a suit. But which suit?

There are three easy rules:

1. Bid a five-card major or a four-card minor, the longer the better.
2. With equal-length suits bid the higher-ranking.
3. Last resort: bid a three-card minor, clubs preferred. Apply these rules to the six hands above:
    (a) Twelve high-card points and one long-suit asset equals 13 points. You have a five-card major, so bid one spade.
    (b) Ten high-card points, one long-suit asset and two assets for the void in hearts. Bid one spade. Six cards is even better than five.
    (c) Ten high-card points, two long-suit assets plus one for the singleton diamond equals 13 points. Bid one spade, the higher-ranking of the two five-card suits.
    (d) Thirteen high-card points. Bid one diamond, a four-card minor. The hearts look good, but you cannot bid them with only four cards.
    (e) Twelve high-card points plus one asset, the singleton spade, equals 13 points. The heart suit is barred (only four of them), so bid one diamond, the higher-ranking of equal-length suits.
    (f) Thirteen high-card points. Bid one club, the last resort. With no five-card major and no four-card minor we have to improvise in a three-card minor. To keep the bidding low we bid one club, not one diamond.

With 13 points or more we must bid something. Remember that a bid of one of a suit is vague: partner will assume somewhere between 13 and 20 points. (Even stronger hands are possible, but very unlikely.)

Now put yourself in partner's shoes. What is he to do opposite a vague bid?

He will bear in mind this obvious general principle of bidding: do not pass if the combined hands could have 26 points; only pass if the combined hands cannot have 26 points.

Suppose that you bid one spade and your partner passes. What should you assume from that?

He is allowing for the possibility that you have 20 points, so with 6 he must do something: the total might be 26. When he passes he must have fewer than 6 points.

If your partner opens with one of a suit the rule therefore is: *bid something with 6 points or more, pass with 5 points or less.*

Before we consider what partner will bid, we must take another look at assets. We warned you that these might gain in value or lose value in the light of the bidding.

Once the bidding is underway you must keep in mind the degree of fit that has been uncovered. If you seem to have a normal fit, your assets have their normal value. With a good fit, their value doubles. With an excellent fit they triple, and so on. If you have a bad fit, or no fit at all, your assets are worthless. In tabular form:

Known Fit	Quality of Fit	Assets
7 cards or fewer	Bad	Worthless
8 cards	Normal	Unchanged
9 cards	Good	Double
10 cards	Excellent	Triple
and so on		

Suppose that your partner opens one spade and you find spades acceptable (you have at least three). You should now be able to judge your prospects.

Your Point Count	Game Chance	Your Bid
0-5	Impossible	Pass
6-9	Unlikely	Two spades
10-12	Likely	Three spades
13+	Certain	Four spades

(Note: The four-spade bid in the table above always relies on assets and never has 13 points in high cards. For more on this, and on the three-spade bid, see page 216, 'Strong raise.' Both bids promise at least four-card support.)

Try this out on these three responding hands. In each case your partner has opened one spade and the next player passes. What do you bid?

a) ♠ K 8 7 5 3   b) ♠ K 8 7 5   c) ♠ Q 9 2
   ♡ —   ♡ 6   ♡ 7 3
   ◊ J 9 3 2   ◊ K 9 3 2   ◊ A 8 7 6 3
   ♣ 7 6 3 2   ♣ K 6 3 2   ♣ 6 3 2

(a) Only 4 high-card points, but what a marvelous fit for partner's spades! Partner has promised five cards in spades, so the partnership total is ten. With an excellent ten-card fit assets triple, so our original three assets (1 for the long spade suit and 2 for the void in hearts) are now 9. Add the 4 high-card points and we have enough, counting on partner for 13, to bid game: bid four spades.

   This bid may gain in more than one way. Even if four spades fails we may find that we have prevented the enemy from reaching a good contract in hearts.

(b) With four spades opposite five we have a good nine-card fit, and assets double. We only have 1, for the singleton heart, so our original 10 points have become 11. Opposite partner's announced 13 points, game is likely but not certain. Bid three spades. This is a strong invitation to partner, who will pass with a minimum opening but continue to game with a little extra strength.

(c) With three spades opposite five we have a normal fit. Our 1 asset, for the long diamond suit, is unchanged, and we have the same 7 points that we began with. Game is possible, since partner might have 19 or 20, but unlikely. Bid two spades.

Now let us go back to the opening bidder. Suppose he has:

♠ A K J 10 5 3   ♡ A J   ◊ K 5   ♣ Q 8 4

He opens one spade holding 18 high-card points and 1 asset. He hears you bid two spades, showing that game is unlikely. The single raise shows 6-9 points and a normal fit.

He has one more spade than he promised originally, and can be sure of a nine-card fit in the combined hands. His 1 asset, for the long spade suit, has therefore doubled and his net worth is 20. The response promised at least 6, so he can count to 26 and bid four spades.

The lead is a small club, and the dummy turns out to be hand (c) above. The declarer is therefore looking at this layout. We will allow you to play the hand for him.

NORTH
♠ Q 9 2
♡ 7 3
◇ A 8 7 6 3
♣ 6 3 2

West leads the club five

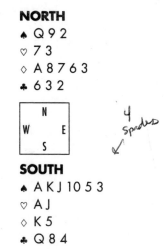

SOUTH
♠ A K J 10 5 3
♡ A J
◇ K 5
♣ Q 8 4

For the first three tricks the defenders are in charge. East wins the first trick with the club ace and returns the suit. You try the queen, without much hope, and West takes the king and plays the jack, which wins the next trick. He then shifts to a small heart, East plays the queen and you win with the ace.

You have lost three tricks, which is all you can afford. You are in great danger of losing a heart trick. How can you avoid this?

There is only one hope, and that is to do something with dummy's diamond suit. If you can find a way to make one of dummy's small diamonds win a trick you can discard your heart jack and make the contract.

Your aim is to establish at least one diamond trick by taking away all the enemy diamonds. But that will not do any good unless you can find a way back to the dummy. You must watch your entries.

Outside diamonds, what entries do you have to the dummy?

The answer is two: the queen and nine of trumps. You must be very careful not to waste them. Save them until they are needed.

There is no harm in playing (or **cashing**) the ace of spades, since that does not take away an entry from the dummy. Both opponents follow suit, and it is time to work on diamonds.

Remember the rule: high from short. So start with the king of diamonds and then lead to the ace. Then play a third diamond, and when East follows suit, trump (or ruff) dramatically with the king of spades. You can afford this, but what you cannot afford is to play a low trump and then find that West can play a higher trump, an **over-ruff**. West discards a heart, foiled of his chance for an overruff.

The position you see is now this:

NORTH
♠ Q 9
♡ 7
◇ 8 7
♣ —

```
      N
   W     E
      S
```

SOUTH
♠ J 10 5 3
♡ J
◇ —
♣ —

Now it is time to use the two entries to dummy that you have loving-ly preserved. Lead a low spade to the nine, noting that West follows and East discards. Then lead a diamond and trump with the spade jack. You have achieved your object: the last diamond in the dummy has become a winner.

Lead a trump to the queen, a play that achieves two purposes. It removes the last of the opponents' trumps, and it gives you an entry to the dummy exactly when you need it. Play the winning diamond and throw away your heart jack. You still have one trump in your hand to take the last trick, giving you your game. Well played!

Just in case you would like to play through the deal again, looking at all four hands, here is the complete layout. (Otherwise jump ahead — or skip ahead — and continue reading.)

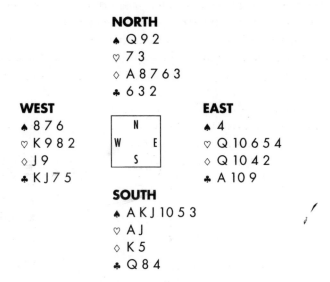

NORTH
♠ Q 9 2
♡ 7 3
♦ A 8 7 6 3
♣ 6 3 2

WEST
♠ 8 7 6
♡ K 9 8 2
♦ J 9
♣ K J 7 5

EAST
♠ 4
♡ Q 10 6 5 4
♦ Q 10 4 2
♣ A 10 9

SOUTH
♠ A K J 10 5 3
♡ A J
♦ K 5
♣ Q 8 4

Before we abandon the subject of descriptive, limited responses to an opening bid of one of a suit, there is one other very important subject (and a few less important ones) we must cover.

Suppose that your partner opens one spade and you respond one notrump. That is the equivalent in strength of a raise to two spades, but it shows an aversion to spades. Your partner will expect you to have the same 6-9 points that you would have for two spades, but fewer than three spades. You cannot see a normal fit in spades, so your assets, if any, have disappeared; your 6-9 points will be high-card points[1].

For an example of the one-notrump response, look back to the diagram of the hand we just played. The North hand would respond one notrump if the opening bid happened to be one heart instead of one spade.

---

1. For a modern use of the 1NT response, see *Scientific Style* on page 213.

The one-notrump response to any other suit means the same, but there is one tricky point: a suit response at the one-level, which is coming in the next lesson, is always preferable, so one notrump denies that possibility. Therefore one notrump in response to one heart denies a four-card spade suit. And one notrump in response to one diamond denies four cards in either major.

Three other descriptive responses are rare but must be mentioned:

1. A jump to two notrump (for example, *one spade-two notrump*) shows opening values (13-15 points), a balanced hand, and something good in each of the unbid suits[2].

2. A jump to three notrump (for example, *one spade-three notrump*) is similar, but the strength is greater, about equal to an opening one notrump.

3. Raises in a minor suit (for example, one diamond-two diamonds or one diamond-three diamonds) are just like raises in a major suit with two provisos: they deny possession of a four-card (or longer) major suit. They show at least four-card support — a normal fit, since opener is very likely to have a four-card suit. (Most of the time the player who raises has five-card support.)

QUIZ

---

1. How many total points, counting high cards and assets, do each of the following hands have?

   a) ♠ A 4
      ♡ A K 7 6 3
      ◊ A J 9 7 4 2
      ♣ —

   b) ♠ A K Q J
      ♡ 10 9 8 7
      ◊ —
      ♣ 10 9 8 7 6

   c) ♠ A K Q J
      ♡ A 4 2
      ◊ A J 2
      ♣ 4 3 2

---

2. For a modern meaning, see *Jacoby Two Notrump* on page 215.

2. As dealer, what would you bid with each of the hands shown in Question 1?

3. If your partner opened one heart, what would you respond with each of the following hands?

a) ♠ 3 2
    ♡ A 9 8 2
    ♢ 8 7 6 3 2
    ♣ 3 2

b) ♠ 4 3 2
    ♡ A 9 8 2
    ♢ K J 7 6 2
    ♣ 5

c) ♠ —
    ♡ J 8 7 6 5 4
    ♢ 4 3 2
    ♣ 7 6 5 4

4. Suppose that you open one heart with the following hand:

     ♠ —   ♡ A J 8 7 6 3 2   ♢ A 3 2   ♣ A 3 2

What will your next move be if your partner responds: (a) two hearts; (b) three hearts.

5. If you plan to establish dummy's long suit, what should your main concern be?

QUIZ ANSWERS

---

1. (a) Twenty points, 16 in high cards and 4 assets. This is the normal maximum for a one-bid.
   (b) Thirteen points, including 3 assets, a minimum for a one-bid.
   (c) Nineteen points. If you remember that ace-king-queen-jack is worth 10, you can count the spade suit quickly and save mental effort.

2. (a) One diamond, because the suit is longer than the hearts.
   (b) One club, the long suit. Spades and hearts are ruled out anyway, since a bid in either major promises at least five cards.
   (c) One club. Too strong for one notrump, so you must use the last-resort bid of a three-card minor suit (clubs rather than diamonds).

3. (a) Two hearts. You can count on a nine-card fit, so your one asset has doubled, giving you exactly the 6 points you need to raise to the two-level, saying game is possible but unlikely.

If your partner had opened one spade you would have had to pass. Your 1 asset would be worthless.

(b) Three hearts. You are enthusiastic about hearts, and know there is a nine-card fit. Your 2 assets double, for a total of 12 points. You have almost enough to bid four hearts, but an invitational jump to three hearts is enough. Partner will not pass unless he has a minimum opening.

(c) Four hearts. You have an incredible fit: eleven cards (conceivably more) in the combined hands. Your 3 assets quadruple to 12 and you can count 26. If your partner had opened one spade you would have passed without hesitation, which proves how much difference a good fit makes.

4. (a) You have 16 points including 3 assets. Your partner's raise to two hearts promises three-card support: he could 'see' a normal fit assuming five hearts in your hand. You now know there is a ten-card fit, so your assets triple. You can count more than enough for a game. Bid four hearts.

(b) Your partner's jump to three hearts suggests four-card heart support and about 11 points. Your three assets have quadrupled. The total is about 36, more than the 33 you need for a small slam. Bid six hearts.

5. If you plan to establish dummy's suit, look carefully for entries. Preserve them lovingly until you need them.

ESSENTIALS TO REMEMBER

1. Assets double with a nine-card fit, triple with a ten-card fit, and so on. They disappear with less than a normal fit.

2. Open with a five-card major or a four-card minor, the longer the better. Bid the higher-ranking of suits with equal length. As a last resort bid a three-card minor, clubs preferred.

3. If you raise your partner one level (one spade-two spades) you show 6-9 points and a normal fit. If you skip a level (one spade-three spades) you show 10-12 with a good fit, inviting game. If you skip two levels (one spade-four spades) you show 13+ including some assets.

4. A one-notrump response is like raising one level (6-9 points) but denies a normal fit. A two notrump response shows the values for an opening bid: it suggests a balanced hand with strength spread around the unbid suits.

5. Be careful about entries to the dummy, especially if you plan to establish and use dummy's long suit.

The search for accurate description goes on. The opener makes an accurate bid of one notrump if he can. If he cannot, he makes a vague opening of one of a suit, hoping that his partner will make an accurate response by raising the opening bid or bidding some number of notrump. Most of the time, however, partner cannot do that and has to answer vagueness with vagueness. A foggy cloud covers the auction, and we have to wait a little longer for the sun to come out. Suppose the bidding starts:

Opener (dealer)	**Responder** (partner)
1♣	1♡

The message carried by one heart is clearly vague: 'I have a few points, perhaps a lot, and a few hearts, perhaps a lot. I cannot describe my hand. Please describe yours.' *— at least 4*

The number of points must be six or more. *)*

As for any other response to a one-opening, six points are needed. With fewer, the chance of 26 combined points is negligible and we simply pass.

Six points is the minimum, but there is no maximum. We could easily have enough to be sure of game, or to be hoping for slam. We have asked opener to describe his hand and he will do so. He will never pass.

The number of hearts must be four or more.

As usual, we are looking for a normal eight-card fit. We respond in a four-card major because there is a good chance that the opener also has four and we will uncover a normal fit.

We may have five hearts, or six hearts, or more. That will appear later: we know we will have another chance to bid.

To sum up: any one-level suit response shows 6 or more points, shows four or more cards in the suit, and is forcing. Opener is not allowed to pass and must describe his hand.

Which suit does responder bid? The rules are rather like those for opening the bidding:

1. Bid the longest suit.
2. Bid the higher-ranking with two five-card suits.
3. Bid cheaply with four-card suits.

Now try these examples. What do you respond to your partner's opening of one club?

a)	♠ A K Q J	b)	♠ 6 5 4 3 2	c)	♠ A Q 3 2
	♡ 3 2		♡ A K Q J 2		♡ 5 4 3 2
	◇ A Q 7 6 5		◇ K 2		◇ 4 3 2
	♣ 3 2		♣ 2		♣ 3 2

(a) Long suit first is the basic rule: bid one diamond. Spades can wait. Your partner cannot pass: one diamond is forcing. (New suits by the responder are in general forcing.) In this case you are thinking about a slam.

(b) Bid one spade. The higher-ranking with two five-card suits is the rule. At your next turn you will bid strongly in hearts, expecting to play game in one of the major suits. The reason for bidding this way, as opener or responder, is to make it easy for partner to choose later: if you bid spades and then hearts he can select spades without having to go to a higher level. With five-card suits, bidding high to begin with keeps it low in the long run.

(c) Bid one heart. With four-card suits bid cheaply. You have barely the 6 points you need to respond at all. You are hoping to find a normal four-four fit in hearts or spades. If partner has hearts you have found it. If he has spades, you give him an easy opportunity to bid that suit.

The suit response asks partner to describe his hand, indeed forces him to do so. How does he do it?

Opener (dealer)	**Responder** (partner)
1♣	1♡
??	

Accurate description is always better than vagueness, so as usual the opener tries to do something descriptive. And as usual, raises (of a major suit) and notrump bids are the first choices.

Strength	Points	Game Chances	
Minimum	13-16	Unlikely	4 cards (perhaps 3)
Strong	17-19	Likely	4 cards 3♡
Maximum	20+	Certain	4 cards 4♡

This closely parallels the raises by responder of an opening bid of one heart (or one spade). A single raise is discouraging, and a jump raise to the three-level is encouraging, suggesting that the combined hands have about 24 points. Partner continues if he has a little in reserve for his previous bid.

Choose your rebid with each of the following. You have opened one club and your partner has responded one heart.

a)	♠ 3	b)	♠ K 4 3	c)	♠ K Q 4 2
	♡ A 8 7		♡ A J 7 2		♡ A Q 10 4
	◇ K 7 6 2		◇ 2		◇ 3
	♣ A 10 9 6 2		♣ A K 7 6 3		♣ A K J 2

(a) Bid two hearts. You cannot be sure of a normal fit, but hearts is promising: partner will probably be able to trump one or two spades in your hand. There is no sensible alternative to two hearts.

In general, a direct raise of partner's suit promises at least four cards. But if a player's first bid is a major suit a single raise is allowable with three cards (one heart-two hearts, or one club-one heart-two hearts).

(b) Bid three hearts. A normal fit is certain, so your 2 assets retain their value, and 17 points is just enough for the encouraging jump. You know that the combined hands have at least 23 points and partner will continue if he possibly can.

(c) Bid four hearts[1]. Your partner promised four hearts and 6 points, so you have a normal fit and can add to 26 combined points. Partner will probably pass, but may head for slam if he is strong.

---

1. You could also bid 4◇ on this hand, a **splinter jump**; see page 216.

...ke an accurate descriptive **rebid**
...e notrump (one club-one heart-one
...nd that was not good enough to start
...nt count must therefore be 13-14, since a
...would have begun with one notrump. Two
...ne heart-two notrump) shows a balanced hand
...o good to open one notrump (that is, 18-20 points).
...ype of rebid for the opener is a bid in a new suit, the
t... ...partnership. This nearly always shows exactly four cards.
Con... ...these four sequences:

a) Opener	Responder	b) Opener	Responder
1◇	1♡	1◇	1♠
1♠		2♣	

c) Opener	Responder	d) Opener	Responder
1◇	1♠	1◇	1♠
2♡		3♣	

All these suggest that the responder choose one of the opener's suits.
If he goes back to the first suit at the cheapest level it is **preference**.
When in doubt, and particularly when he likes the opener's suits
equally well because he himself has equal length in them, the responder returns to the first-bid suit.

The first two sequences are in principle weak (although they may
have some strength in reserve) because preference is easy. Notice that
the responder does not have to go beyond the two-level to bid diamonds: he can bid only two diamonds in each case. In (b) the opener is likely to have five diamonds, since he spurned a chance to show
a balanced hand by bidding one notrump.

In (c) and (d) cheap preference is not possible, so the opener has
shown a strong hand. Without a jump, as in (c), the bid is called a
reverse and indicates a hand with at least 17 points. The **jump shift**
rebid in (d) guarantees a game and promises about 20 points.

Finally, and normally the last choice, is the rebid of the opener's suit.

a) Opener	Responder	b) Opener	Responder
1◇	1♠	1◇	1♠
2◇		3◇	

In each case the opener shows at least six diamonds and incidentally denies possession of four spades. In (a) he has a minimum hand, with at most 16 high-card points. In (b) he is likely to have 17-19.

Here is a rebid table, assuming that the opening bid was one diamond and the response one spade:

Approx. strength (including assets)	16 maximum	17-19	20+
Raise	2♠	3♠	4♠
Support	(3 or 4 cards)	(4 cards)	(4 cards)
Notrump	1NT (13-14)	2NT (18-20)	3NT*
New suit	2♣ (perhaps stronger)	2♡ (reverse)	3♣ (jump shift)

*This is a rare rebid. It shows very long solid diamonds and stoppers in hearts and clubs.

The situations we have discussed refer to responses at the one-level. If the suit response has to be made at the two-level, as it always does after a one-spade opening and sometimes does after a red-suit opening, the hand must be stronger: a two-over-one response shows at least 10 high-card points[2].

If the responder bids a major suit (one spade-two hearts), the suit must be five cards in length. A minor-suit response (for example, one spade-two clubs) may be a four-card suit.

The responder follows the usual rules for choosing his suit.

Now let us turn from theory to practice. You deal yourself this hand:

♠ K 10 4   ♡ 6 2   ◇ A K Q 3   ♣ Q 7 6 2

What do you bid?

---

2. But see *Scientific Style* on page 213.

The right call is one diamond. With 14 points you are not quite strong enough for one notrump. With equal-length suits you bid the higher-ranking.

Your partner responds with one spade. What do you do now? You might bid one notrump, and some players would, but two spades is slightly better: you are very weak in hearts for notrump purposes. This is the one situation in which a three-card raise is permitted. *Four-card support is mandatory for a jump raise of a major suit, a raise of a minor suit, or a raise of partner's second suit.*

Your partner now bids three spades. So the bidding has been:

You	Partner
1♢	1♠
2♠	3♠

If your partner felt sure of 26 combined points he would bid four spades. If he felt that 26 was impossible he would pass two spades. Therefore he thinks game is possible, and he is inviting you to continue if you have a little in reserve.

You do have something in reserve: your opening bid promised 13 points and you have 14. So you bid four spades, ending the bidding.

West leads the jack of diamonds and you put down your dummy. As we are just practicing, you can come round the table and play the hand for your partner. You see this:

NORTH
♠ K 10 4
♡ 6 2
♢ A K Q 3
♣ Q 7 6 2

West leads the diamond jack

```
      N
   W     E
      S
```

SOUTH
♠ A Q J 9 2
♡ J 8 5 4
♢ 8 6
♣ K 5

Notice that South has 12 points, including one asset. When you showed 13-16 with your raise to two spades he was in doubt about 26 points. So he invited you, showing that he could count to about 25 in the combined hands.

In a suit contract it is usually best to count losers. We are completely safe in spades and diamonds, and we have one sure loser in clubs. We appear to be in danger of losing three or four heart tricks, but there is a saving clause: if hearts are played three times we can trump in the dummy.

Try the opposite side of the coin and look at winners. We have five spade tricks, three diamond tricks, and one club trick. Where can we find the tenth trick?

There are no more tricks to be had in diamonds, nor in clubs unless the defenders make a mistake and allow you to score the king and the queen. So we must focus on hearts.

If the opponents played hearts it would be helpful. But if they do not you must. So win the first trick with the diamond queen and lead a heart. Whatever the defenders do you will then lead another heart. And eventually you will trump at least one heart in the dummy.

It would be a terrible error for you to lead any trumps, because you need dummy's trumps. The whole deal is:

NORTH
♠ K 10 4
♡ 6 2
◊ A K Q 3
♣ Q 7 6 2

WEST
♠ 8 7 6
♡ A Q 3
◊ J 10 9 7
♣ J 9 4

EAST
♠ 5 3
♡ K 10 9 7
◊ 5 4 2
♣ A 10 8 3

SOUTH
♠ A Q J 9 2
♡ J 8 5 4
◊ 8 6
♣ K 5

This deal illustrates a basic principle, giving guidance in a vital area: when to **draw trumps** – that is, play your own high trumps to remove any trumps the opponents hold.

In general, if you can see a non-trump suit in which you have more cards in your hand than in the dummy, postpone drawing trumps. If you cannot see such a suit, tend to draw trumps at once.

In the deal we have just played, we have more hearts in our hand than in dummy. This suggests the possibility of ruffing (trumping) a heart in the dummy to gain a trick. We keep leading hearts, and we do not touch trumps. It will suit the opponents to lead trumps, but unless they do it right at the start they will be too late to stop you.

Ruffing in dummy normally helps you because dummy is usually the short trump hand so a ruff produces a trick. Ruffing in your own hand, usually the long trump hand, seldom does any good and tends to be a mistake.

It is important to keep track of the number of trumps the opponents have. Most players try to count all the trumps that are played and often arrive at the wrong answer.

There is an easy way: at the start of the play count the number of trumps the opponents hold. If you have a normal fit, this will be five. Then mentally reduce that number as the opponents play their trumps. Do not include your trumps in the count: that is unnecessary and confusing.

QUIZ

1. If your partner opens one club, what should you respond with each of the following hands?

   a) ♠ A Q 4 3
       ♡ 4
       ◇ A 5 2
       ♣ K J 8 7 4

   b) ♠ A 8 7 2
       ♡ A 8 7 2
       ◇ A 8 7 2
       ♣ J

   c) ♠ 4 3
       ♡ 9 8 7 3 2
       ◇ A K Q 3 2
       ♣ 4

2. If you open one club and your partner responds one spade, what should you rebid with each of the following hands?

a) ♠ K 4 3   b) ♠ K Q J 3   c) ♠ 4 3
   ♡ A 7 6 2   ♡ —   ♡ A Q 3
   ◊ Q 6 5   ◊ A 4 3   ◊ K J 2
   ♣ K J 4   ♣ A Q J 4 3 2   ♣ A K J 10 4

3. If you open one spade and your partner responds two hearts, what do you expect him to have?

4. As South you play four spades with each of the following layouts. Would you plan to draw trumps at once or not?

a)
NORTH
♠ K J 4
♡ A 7 6 3 2
◊ A 3
♣ 5 4 2

SOUTH
♠ A Q 10 5 2
♡ 8 4
◊ K 8 2
♣ A 10 6

b)
NORTH
♠ K J 4
♡ A 7 6 3 2
◊ A 3
♣ 5 4 2

SOUTH
♠ A Q 10 5 2
♡ Q 8 4
◊ K 8
♣ A 10 6

1. (a) One spade. First find out if partner can support spades. There is no hurry to support clubs. We plan to play game, but it is unlikely to be in clubs. Direct support for a minor denies interest in the major suits.

   (b) One diamond. Bid cheaply with four-card suits, giving partner an easy opportunity to show another suit. (One heart is acceptable, but one spade is wrong.)

   (c) One heart. Bid the higher-ranking with five-card suits. We are hoping for a normal fit in hearts. Diamonds can wait.

2. (a) One notrump, showing a balanced hand that was not strong enough to open one notrump. With no chance of a ruff this would be the wrong time to raise spades with three cards.

   (b) Four spades[3]. We are sure of a normal fit, so our three assets retain their value and we can add to 26 combined points.

   (c) Two notrump. Showing a balanced hand that was slightly too good to open one notrump originally.

3. At least five hearts and at least 10 high-card points.

4. (a) Do not draw trumps. You have more diamonds in your hand than in the dummy, so your plan is to trump a diamond after taking the ace and king. That gives you ten tricks. You lose one heart trick and two clubs.

   (b) Draw trumps. You have no suit in which you are longer than dummy (not counting trumps), so you have no chance of a useful ruff. Plan to work on hearts. Your best chance is that East has the heart king, and you can score the queen by leading toward that card.

---

3. But see *splinter* on page 216.

ESSENTIALS TO REMEMBER

As Responder

1. A new-suit response at the one-level shows 6 or more points, at the two-level 10 or more high-card points. Both are forcing, asking opener to describe his hand. Both may be very strong.

2. Respond in your long suit. Bid the higher-ranking with two five-card suits. Bid cheaply with two or more four-card suits.

As Opener

3. Raise the response one level with a minimum hand, two levels with a strong hand. If you can see game, bid it. Support usually shows four cards, but three is possible for a single raise in a major.

4. A minimum notrump rebid shows a minimum balanced opening. A jump notrump rebid shows a hand too good for an original one notrump.

5. A new-suit rebid can be weak if responder can return to the original suit at the two-level. If not, it is either a reverse, a non-jump action inviting game, or a jump shift, guaranteeing game.

6. A rebid of opener's suit shows at least six cards. Without a jump it shows a minimum. With a jump it is invitational.

7. In choosing a rebid, think about strength and distribution. The usual order of preference is: raise; notrump; new suit; original suit.

As Declarer

8. Look for a chance to ruff in the dummy. (Dummy must be shorter in the suit you plan to ruff.) If you see such a chance it is usually right to play for the ruff before drawing trumps.

9. Count the opponents' trumps when the play starts and then keep track of them. Do not count your own trumps.

It is time to learn the Golden Rule of bidding: <u>bidding a suit twice shows six cards or more</u>. For example:

Opener	Responder
1♡	1♠
2♡	

The logic of this is obvious. The opener has already promised five cards in hearts with his opening bid and would be foolish to give the same message again. With only five hearts he will always have a better alternative: bid one notrump, support spades, or bid a minor suit.

Many players think that they ought to rebid a minor suit to show five cards but that is quite wrong. It is much more important to give new information rather than to stress something already known.

The Rule applies to major suits and minor suits, to the opening bidder and the responder (there are two small exceptions: your own second suit and a suit that partner has supported). When your partner does rebid his suit, you can build confidently on that information. Suppose you have this hand:

♠ A J 7 6 4　♡ K 2　◇ 3 2　♣ Q 10 5 2

Partner	You
1♡	1♠
2♡	

The bidding has gone as shown above: You have responded in spades, and your partner has <u>rebid</u> his hearts. What do you bid?

Since your partner knows the Golden Rule, he must have at least six hearts. That gives you a normal fit, so your one asset keeps its value.

must have 6 to rebid

Your hand is worth 11, and your partner's rebid has shown a minimum opening, probably 13-16. You can add to 24 and there is a chance of 26. You therefore bid three hearts, inviting partner to continue with a little extra.

If your hand were a little stronger, with 13 points, you would bid four hearts, which is an example of a general principle: *if you can add to 26 combined points you must either bid a game or make a forcing bid.*

In other words, if you know there is a game do not give your partner a chance to pass before you get there.

Now we must go back to the one-over-one suit response:

Opener	Responder
1♣	1♡
(13+)	(6+)

Both players have made vague bids. We have seen three ways in which the opener with a minimum hand can give an accurate description at this point:

1. He can bid two hearts (usually four-card support, but perhaps three).

2. He can bid one notrump, showing a hand not good enough to bid one notrump originally.

3. He can rebid his suit (two clubs), showing six or more cards. (Three clubs would show a better hand, with about 17 high-card points.)

He can also make a third vague bid, preserving the fog, by bidding one spade. This suggests a four-card spade suit but says very little about strength. (It does deny the ability to guarantee a game. With 20 points, or perhaps 19, the bid would be two spades.) The buck is passed again, and the responder will try to describe his hand. He has many ways to do that, and all it takes is a little common sense.

Remember that the bidding has gone:

Opener	Responder
1♣	1♡
1♠	??

With a very weak responding hand, in the 6-9-point range, the responder has several options.

(a) *Pass.* Very weak: 6 or 7 points, and probably three spades. (Remember: a new suit by responder is forcing, but a new suit by opener is not.)

(b) *Two clubs.* A weak preference bid, with more clubs than spades.

(c) *Two hearts.* A weak hand with six or more hearts (the Golden Rule).

(d) *Two spades.* Four-card support, finding a normal fit, because it is opener's second suit and he is practically certain to have only four cards in it, not five.

(e) *One notrump.* No fit for opener's suits. Some length or strength in the unbid diamond suit and 6-9 high-card points.

Those five options are all precise descriptive moves showing that game is unlikely. They allow the responder to dispel the fog when he is weak.

When he is slightly stronger, in the 10-12-point range, he is entitled to feel that game is likely. He can see about 24 points in the combined hands but not 26. He issues an invitation by making a jump bid. Barring a jump in a new suit, which would guarantee game, he has the following options:

(f) *Three spades.* This shows 10-12 points and four-card spade support. A normal fit, so assets keep their value.

(g) *Three hearts.* This shows 10-12 points and a six-card heart suit (the Golden Rule). No normal fit in sight, so assets are worthless.

(h) *Three clubs.* This shows 10-12 points and at least four-card club support.

(i) *Two notrump.* This shows 10-12 points in high cards, including some strength in the unbid diamond suit. No normal fit is available, so assets are worthless. Note that two notrump is almost always an invitational, encouraging bid, whether made with a jump or not. For example:

Opener	Responder
1 ♡	1 ♠
2 ♣	2NT

The two notrump bid shows about 11 points with something in the unbid suit.

Finally, we have to consider what the responder does with a hand on which he can count 26 combined points or more and therefore wishes to insist on game. Usually he will simply go right ahead and bid game[1].

(j) *Four spades.* This shows 13-16 points and exactly four spades. A normal fit, so assets are stable.

(k) *Three notrump.* This shows 13-16 points, with some strength in the unbid diamond suit. No normal fit is available, so assets are worthless.

(l) *Four hearts.* This shows 13-16 points with no normal fit, so assets are worthless. Strong emphasis on hearts when opener is probably short, so a seven-card suit is likely.

It is not necessary to remember all these possible bids, but try to understand the logic behind them. A useful exercise is to take a deck and construct a hand on which the opener will bid one club and rebid one spade (which incidentally denies four-card heart support). Then construct random responding hands that include a heart suit and select the right bid on the second round.

Here is an easy example; you are sitting South:

♠ 10 7 4   ♡ A K Q J   ◊ A 6 2   ♣ 7 5 4

As usual, your partner has opened one club and you have responded one heart. He has rebid one spade. What do you do now?

With 14 high-card points opposite an opening bid you are sure of the combined 26 needed for game. There does not appear to be a normal fit in a major: partner cannot have four hearts, since he would have raised if he did, and is wildly unlikely to have five spades. So you bid three notrump, showing a desire to play that contract. A notrump bid on the second or third round of

---

1. For an advanced move by which the responder can maintain the fog, see page 214, *Fourth suit.*

bidding virtually guarantees some strength in any unbid suit. We therefore promise something in diamonds. (Note that with a slightly weaker hand, worth about 11 points, we would bid two notrump to invite game.)

Partner passes, West leads his long suit, a diamond, and the layout turns out to be:

NORTH
♠ K J 5 3
♡ 7 2
◇ Q 9
♣ A K 9 8 2

West leads the diamond four

SOUTH
♠ 10 7 4
♡ A K Q J
◇ A 6 2
♣ 7 5 4

Counting winners should be your first thought in notrump. (In a suit contract, losers are your primary concern.) You have seven sure winners and need two more. You may get an extra diamond trick, and you could work on spades to develop a trick, but your best chance is certainly in clubs.

Your *longest combined suit* is usually the right one to develop in notrump. Here this is clubs, and we must analyze the prospects.

How many clubs do the opponents have?

Five.

How would you expect the five to be divided?

Three in one hand and *two* in the other. *An odd number of cards tends to divide evenly.* (An even number of cards tends to divide unevenly: six cards are more likely to split four-two than three-three.)

So how many additional club tricks can we hope for?

Two in addition to the ace and king.

How many club tricks can the opponents make, assuming a normal three-two split?

One. If the ace and king are played, they will have one winning card remaining.

We said earlier that a five-card suit offers the possibility of five tricks. Here you are sure to make two tricks, and you expect to take two more eventually with small cards. You take four tricks and the enemy one: total, five.

Bear this in mind as we play the hand. The first decision to be made involves the diamond suit. Should we play the queen from dummy or not?

The best chance to take a trick with the queen is to play it at once in the hope that West has the king. Unfortunately when we play the queen East covers with the king.

Should we take the ace?

Certainly not.

There are two general principles involved here, and they are two sides of the same coin.

1. Do not be in a hurry to take sure winners in a key suit, whether your suit or the enemy suit.

2. Tricks that must be lost should usually be lost quickly.

So save your winning diamond as long as possible, and let them take immediately the diamond tricks that you know you must lose.

When you **hold up** your ace, allowing the king to win, East leads the diamond jack. Obviously the defenders will persevere with their long suit. You hold up your ace again, and finally take it on the third round of the suit.

Your hold-up play had a vital effect. At this point West has two winning diamonds but as the cards lie (see the diagram of this deal below) he has no way to gain the lead. If you had taken your diamond ace prematurely East would still have been able to lead a diamond if he gained the lead.

Now you must carry out your main plan, which is to establish dummy's clubs.

Following the two principles we have just stated, you lead a club and when West plays low you try the nine (or the eight) from the dummy.

You expect to lose the trick, and you do. East wins with the ten. Your play was a **duck**, a move that deliberately concedes a trick that could have been won.

Your duck has served a double purpose. You have lost the club trick that you knew you would have to lose eventually and kept your line of communication open to the dummy. And at the same time you have lost the lead to East, who is unlikely to have any more diamonds, since eleven have been played and diamonds is West's long suit.

If West had the ace of spades as an entry you would be in trouble. But luckily East has that card and is helpless. He will probably lead a heart now and you will happily take nine tricks: four in hearts and four in clubs to go with your diamond ace.

The complete deal was this:

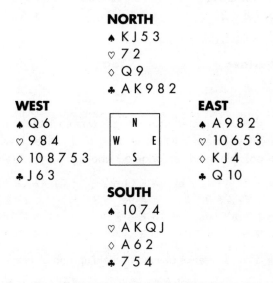

NORTH
♠ K J 5 3
♡ 7 2
◊ Q 9
♣ A K 9 8 2

WEST
♠ Q 6
♡ 9 8 4
◊ 10 8 7 5 3
♣ J 6 3

EAST
♠ A 9 8 2
♡ 10 6 5 3
◊ K J 4
♣ Q 10

SOUTH
♠ 10 7 4
♡ A K Q J
◊ A 6 2
♣ 7 5 4

If you are not quite sure you understand what happened, take a deck and sort the cards as shown. Then play trick by trick. You will see that West's potential diamond tricks were shut out by your hold-up play.

Both the hold-up and the duck concede a trick that could have been won. But the objectives are quite different.

The hold-up calls for a delay in taking a sure trick in the enemy suit. You want to make it harder for them to take their potential tricks.

The duck requires you to lose quickly a trick in a suit in which you have prospects. The main idea is to preserve your entries until you need them.

1. If you open the bidding with one diamond and your partner responds one spade, what should you rebid with each of the following hands?

   a) ♠ K 2.
       ♡ 4 3
       ◇ A K Q 7 2
       ♣ 9 8 4 3

   b) ♠ K 2
       ♡ 4
       ◇ A K Q 7 6 2
       ♣ A J 7 2

   c) ♠ A Q 2
       ♡ 4
       ◇ A K Q 7 6
       ♣ A J 7 2

2. Suppose the bidding starts:

Partner	You
1♣	1♡
1♠	??

   What should you rebid as responder with each of the following hands? (If you need a little help, refer back to the classification of the possible rebids on page 59 above.)

   a) ♠ 4 2
       ♡ K Q 7 6 3
       ◇ K 5 4 2
       ♣ 7 5

   b) ♠ K Q 6 2
       ♡ K 9 7 6 3
       ◇ K 5 2
       ♣ 4

   c) ♠ Q 6 2
       ♡ K Q J 9 6 4
       ◇ K 10 4
       ♣ 4

3. What is the difference between a hold-up and a duck?

4. Suppose you are playing three notrump, and dummy has strength in clubs, and only in clubs. What is your plan if you need club tricks and the club suit looks like this:

   a) **Dummy**
       ♣ A K 4 3 2

       You
       ♣ 7 6

   b) **Dummy**
       ♣ A 8 7 3 2

       You
       ♣ K 5 4

   c) **Dummy**
       ♣ A 8 7 3 2

       You
       ♣ 9 5 4

1. (a) Two clubs. Your partner's bid was forcing, and the most help-
       ful thing you can do is to show your second suit. That it is weak
       is not important: as you have refused to bid one notrump your
       partner will know that your hand is unbalanced. He will expect
       you to have five diamonds and four or five clubs. If he prefers
       diamonds, or likes your suits equally, he will bid two dia-
       monds. That is a preference bid and is weak. He will only pass
       two clubs if he has more clubs than diamonds. He might have
       many more: perhaps five clubs and only one diamond. Then
       clubs will be an ideal contract.

       One notrump is the second-best bid, but the weakness in
       hearts is menacing. The bid that is totally wrong is two dia-
       monds. That would break the Golden Rule and invite disaster.

    (b) Three diamonds. When opener rebids his suit with a jump he
       shows about 17 high-card points and at least a six-card suit
       (the Golden Rule again). Since there is no indication of a nor-
       mal fit your original two assets have become worthless.
       Second choice: two clubs. Three diamonds is a strong invita-
       tion, but not forcing.

    (c) Three clubs. The only way, short of bidding game, for the open-
       er to show a combined 26 points is to jump in a new suit.
       Three clubs guarantees game, so partner must do something.
       Your plan is to support spades next: Delayed support usually
       shows exactly three cards, for with four you would support
       immediately.

2. (a) One notrump. Showing a weak hand and a dislike for part-
       ner's suits. This suggests some length or strength in the unbid
       diamond suit. You cannot pass one spade, for partner proba-
       bly has four and you would be outnumbered in trumps. Two
       hearts would clearly be wrong, breaking the Golden Rule.

    (b) Four spades. When partner opened one club there was no fit
       in sight and your two assets became worthless. But now you
       know there is a normal spade fit, four in each hand, and the

assets come back to life. You have 13 points in all, which gives 26 when combined with partner's 13 for his opening bid. You are a fraction too strong for three spades, which would be an invitation. Partner might pass that.

(c) Three hearts. There is no normal fit in sight, so our assets are worthless. We have 11 high-card points, which justifies an invitation to game. We are too strong for a weak bid of two hearts, and not strong enough to insist on playing a game. Partner will know we have six hearts (the Golden Rule again).

3. A hold-up is a maneuver in the enemy suit, waiting to take a sure trick in the hope of cutting their communications. A duck is a maneuver in your suit, giving up a trick to increase your long-term prospects in the suit.

4. (a) Duck a trick immediately. When you regain the lead, play your remaining club to the king. Follow with the ace. If you are lucky both opponents will follow to three rounds and the two remaining clubs in the dummy will be winners.

(b) It is vital to save dummy's ace until the third round of the suit. Duck a trick quickly, and hope that the five clubs the opponents own split three-two. They usually will, and you can end up making two extra tricks in the dummy with small cards. (It does not matter whether you play the king immediately or not, but you must keep the ace as an entry.)

(c) This is like (b), but this time the opponents have two sure tricks. Duck a trick, and later duck again. With a normal three-two split you will be able to take the ace eventually and score two more tricks with small clubs.

ESSENTIALS TO REMEMBER

1. Do not bid a five-card suit twice (exceptions: if it is your second suit, or if partner has shown support).

2. If the first three bids are in three different suits, all is fog. Responder will try to dispel it by: (a) any low-level bid with 6-9 points; (b) any jump bid to show 10-12 and invite game; (c) bidding game, if he knows which game to play. (New suit bids are exceptions; see page 214, Fourth suit.)

3. Usually hold up, particularly in notrump, with a sure trick in the enemy suit (unless some other suit is more dangerous).

4. If you know you must lose a trick or two in the suit you want to establish, think about a duck. Conceding a trick early will often help you with your entries.

Slams are the high drama of bridge, with thousands of points riding on good decisions in the bidding, play, and defense. For most players a slam is the high point of an evening of play. There are likely to be one or two of them, generating triumph or disaster, Kipling's two impostors.

As we have seen, a small slam, needing twelve of the thirteen tricks, requires 33 combined points. A grand slam, needing all thirteen, requires 37. But these are minimum values, and there is more to it than that.

A small slam is worth bidding if it has a fifty-fifty chance or better. You stand to gain a large bonus, but if you fail you have lost the game that you could have collected by being more cautious. You need to be rather more sure of your ground if you bid a grand slam, even though the bonus is much bigger. If you fail by one trick you have lost the value of a small slam as well as the game.

There are three common ways to head for slam, each appropriate in different circumstances.

1. DIRECT SLAM-BIDDING

If both hands are balanced and the count is right, bid the slam immediately: one notrump-six notrump, or one notrump-seven notrump. Or an invitation can be issued and accepted: one notrump-four notrump-six notrump.

Suppose you deal yourself this hand:

♠ A K 8 7 4 2   ♡ A 10 7 3   ◇ A 8 4   ♣ —

You bid one spade and your partner responds three spades. You will recall that this is an invitation to game, with the equivalent of about 11 points.

What should you bid now?

Answer: six spades.

Your partner's jump raise promised four-card support, so you have at least ten spades between you. This is an excellent fit, and your assets triple, from 3 to 9. Your count becomes 24, and when you add your partner's 11 you are over the 33-point mark for six spades.

A cautionary note is needed here. *To bid a direct slam, you must be sure that you cannot lose the first two tricks.*

This is true with the hand shown. You know, in fact, that you cannot lose the first trick, let alone the first two.

It is also substantially true if you bid six notrump by counting points. If you have 33 combined high-card points, the opponents have at most 7. They cannot in principle have two aces worth 8 points and the chance that they will take the first two tricks is negligible.

If your combined count seems adequate for a small slam but there is some danger of losing the first two tricks some probing is called for.

2. BLACKWOOD

There are times when it is helpful to ignore the natural meaning of a bid, and agree with your partner that it should be used to convey a different message entirely[1]. This is called a convention. The world's most famous bridge convention, named for the Indianapolis expert who invented it, is quite simple. A bid of four notrump (unless a raise of notrump) asks a question: how many aces do you have, partner?

The answers are made on the step principle:

No ace	5♣
One ace	5♢
Two aces	5♡
Three aces	5♠

---

1. Note that bridge is a game of courtesy and complete disclosure. When you and your partner use a bidding convention, the opponents must be made aware that your bids no longer carry their natural meaning. Some conventions, like the one we are about to describe, are so widespread that usually no explanation will be necessary.

After partner's response to four notrump, five notrump asks for kings in the same way, aiming for a grand slam. This part of the convention is seldom useful.

Here is an illustration of a hand for Blackwood. You deal yourself:

♠ A K 8 7 6 4 2   ♡ 2   ◇ 2   ♣ A K J 2

You bid one spade and your partner bids three spades. You know he has at least four spades and about 11 points. You know that there is an eleven-card spade fit, so your original three assets have quadrupled to 12. Your count is 27, so the combined count is more than enough for a slam.

The only danger is that the opponents, who have about 14 points in high cards, might have both the red aces. You want to ask your partner how many aces he has, and Blackwood is the perfect solution. Bid four notrump.

If your partner has no ace he will bid five clubs. You will know that the opponents have both the red aces, so you bid five spades and partner passes. (He *must* pass: you are in charge of the bidding.) Your partner's dummy will have a bunch of kings and queens, and you are practically certain to make exactly eleven tricks. Playing a contract of five hearts or five spades is generally undesirable, but there is very little risk here.

If your partner bids five diamonds you will know he has one ace. You then bid six spades, and you will have an excellent chance to make twelve tricks. At the worst you might have to take a finesse in clubs, hoping that the queen is on your right.

Suppose now that your partner bids five hearts. This shows that he has both the missing aces. A bid of six spades would be safe, but seven spades would be a worthwhile gamble. Partner might have the club queen. Or he might be short in clubs, in which case you can trump both your jack and two of clubs. And if the worst comes to the worst you can try the club finesse, a fifty-fifty chance.

Notice that the table of responses does not include a bid for when you hold four aces. You can play for years without needing that response, since it means that partner is trying for a slam with an aceless hand. However, if you do have four aces, the response is not, as you might think, five notrump, but five clubs. Partner can always tell whether the number of aces you have is none or four.

Blackwood is intended primarily for situations in which you have sufficient combined values, have selected a suit, but are worried about aces.

There are two situations in which Blackwood is totally unsuitable: *do not use Blackwood with a void (or blank) suit, and do not use Blackwood when the opponents might take the first two tricks in an unbid suit.*

To explain this we must go on to the third method of heading for slam.

3. CUEBIDDING

Consider this bidding:

Opener	Responder
1♠	4♠
5♣	

Obviously we plan to play a spade contract. So what is the point of bidding clubs? Five clubs is a **cuebid**[2], showing that the opener has some control of a side suit, in this case clubs, probably the ace. He is suggesting a slam in spades. He invites partner to cooperate by bidding six spades or by making a similar cuebid in another suit.

This gives us a way to bid toward slam when Blackwood is unsuitable. If you have a void suit, you do not need the ace in partner's hand and Blackwood will not solve your problem. And a weak unbid suit, missing the ace and king, is another situation in which a cuebid is the right approach.

If your partner does not like the slam suggestion he will **sign off** by returning to the agreed trump suit at the cheapest level. In the sequence shown he would bid five spades to show he wanted to stop.

Now it is time to play. Your partner deals and bids one diamond. Your hand is:

♠ A Q   ♡ A K J 8 7 4   ◇ 7 2   ♣ K J 10

---

2. The modern term is **control-bid.**

Assume that you bid one heart[3], asking your partner to describe his hand further.

Your partner bids two hearts, showing three- or four-card heart support and a minimum hand in the 13-16 range. Now estimate the slam prospects. You know there is a nine-card heart fit, so your 1 asset has doubled — it is now worth 2. Add your 18 high-card points and your partner's announced 13 and the total is 33: just enough for a small slam.

A direct bid of six hearts is therefore reasonable. But there is no need to run the risk that two aces are missing. Bid four notrump, Blackwood. Note that the weakness in diamonds is not a serious danger, because partner has bid the suit.

Partner bids five diamonds, showing one ace, and we bid six hearts. If you bid Blackwood and find that the partnership has three or four aces, you should always bid a slam. If three aces are not enough, then you were wrong to bid Blackwood in the first place. Think of Blackwood not as a way of getting to slam but as a way of staying out of it when aces are in short supply.

West leads a club, and you have to play six hearts with this layout:

NORTH
♠ K J
♡ Q 10 5 3
◇ A Q J 10
♣ 6 5 2

West leads the club seven

SOUTH
♠ A Q
♡ A K J 8 7 4
◇ 7 2
♣ K J 10

---

3. There would be nothing wrong, incidentally, with a bid of two hearts. That would show a good suit and interest in slam. The outcome of the auction would be similar.

Before playing from the dummy you carry out the usual survey of your prospects. Everything is under control in the major suits, but there are problems in the minors. You are sure to lose to the club ace, and you are in danger of losing a second club trick and a diamond trick. This will be a hand to draw trumps, since there are no potential ruffs in the dummy.

You play a low club from dummy and East wins with the ace. He returns a club and you must make a decision. You could play the club jack, finessing in the hope that East has the queen. Then you have to finesse later in diamonds, hoping that West has the king.

Finesses are rather like pills. You should take as few as possible, and avoid them altogether if you can.

The chance that two finesses will work, one in clubs and one in diamonds, is poor (one chance in four). You should look for a better plan.

Suppose you refuse to take the club finesse and put up the king, then draw trumps and finesse in diamonds. If that fails you were doomed whatever you did. But if it succeeds you are safe. You reenter your hand with a spade lead and repeat the diamond finesse. Then you can discard your remaining club on the diamond ace.

Taking one finesse is better than taking two. You should pin your hopes on the diamond finesse, which cannot be avoided. The club finesse is a snare and delusion.

The whole deal was:

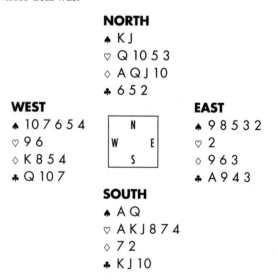

NORTH
♠ K J
♡ Q 10 5 3
♢ A Q J 10
♣ 6 5 2

WEST
♠ 10 7 6 5 4
♡ 9 6
♢ K 8 5 4
♣ Q 10 7

EAST
♠ 9 8 5 3 2
♡ 2
♢ 9 6 3
♣ A 9 4 3

SOUTH
♠ A Q
♡ A K J 8 7 4
♢ 7 2
♣ K J 10

If West had led a spade your plan would have been the same: finesse in diamonds, not clubs. You would have had a little luck. After two finesses the diamond king would have fallen under the ace, avoiding any problem in the club suit. Two clubs from your hand would be discarded on diamonds, and one club trick would be lost eventually.

While we are on the subject of finesses, let us look at a few more finessing situations.

(a) **Dummy**	(b) **Dummy**	(c) **Dummy**	(d) **Dummy**
A Q 10	K J 2	A Q 9	A J 9
You	**You**	**You**	**You**
4 3 2	5 4 3	4 3 2	4 3 2

In each case you plan to lead low to high, from your low cards toward the strength in the dummy. But what card do you play from the dummy?

(a) The ten, intending to finesse the queen later. This gives you a chance to score three tricks if West has the king and jack. If East has both those crucial cards you will only take one trick. And if each opponent has one honor you will take two tricks however you finesse.

(b) The jack, intending to lead towards the king later. This gives you two tricks if you are lucky enough to find both ace and queen on your left. If right-hand opponent has one of the missing honors you will make one trick, and you will make none if both the vital cards are on your right.

(c) The nine, intending to finesse the queen later. If the king is on your left you will take two tricks whether you finesse the queen now or later. Playing the nine has a small advantage: you will make two tricks when West has both the jack and ten, and East has the king.

(d) The nine, hoping to force the queen or king. If that works you will finesse the jack later. This plan succeeds when West has king-ten or queen-ten. Playing the jack at once only works when West has king-queen.

Can you see a pattern to these answers? They follow this useful guideline: *when in doubt, finesse the cheapest plausible card.*

1. Suppose the bidding starts like this:

Partner	You
1♣	1♡
3♡	??

    What should you bid with each of the following hands?

a)	♠ 5	b)	♠ 5 3	c)	♠ 5 3
	♡ A K 8 7 2		♡ A K 8 7 2		♡ A K 8 7 2
	◇ A J 9 6 2		◇ A J 9 6 2		◇ A 9 6 2
	♣ 7 4		♣ 7		♣ 7 4

2. How would you plan to play these suit combinations?

(a) **Dummy**	(b) **Dummy**	(c) **Dummy**
Q 10 2	A K J 9 8 7 6	A 3 2
You	**You**	**You**
5 4 3	2	Q 10 9

3. What are the two warning signals that would discourage you from using Blackwood?

1. Partner's bidding showed 17-19 points with four-card heart support.

    (a) Four notrump. You know there is a nine-card fit, so your 3 assets have doubled. That gives you 18 for a combined 37, more than enough. Before bidding six hearts you might as well use Blackwood to verify that the opponents do not have two aces, although that is very unlikely. Second choice: a direct six hearts. Notice that you are not afraid of clubs, since partner has bid them. There are too many high cards missing to consider a grand slam.

(b) Four diamonds. You would like to bid a slam, but the spade suit is a dangerous weakness. This cuebid, showing the ace of diamonds, invites six hearts. Partner will infer a weakness in spades and act accordingly.

(c) Four hearts. Your one asset has doubled, giving you 13. That does not give you a combined 33, so you should not consider slam.

2. (a) Lead to the ten, finessing the lowest plausible card. You hope that there is ace-jack or king-jack on your left, in which case you can score the queen later by leading toward it.

(b) Finesse the jack. This gains when West has three cards including the queen. This is more likely than finding East with a doubleton queen. A missing honor is more likely to be in a long holding than a short holding.

(c) Lead any card from your hand and play low from dummy if West's card is not higher than the one you lead – a different kind of finesse. Repeat this later, hoping that West has the king, or the jack, or both. The play that is wrong is to start with the ace, giving you a guess next time. (Leading low from dummy is also good, however.)

3. Avoid Blackwood if you have a void suit, or if you have an unbid suit missing the ace and king.

ESSENTIALS TO REMEMBER

1. Consider a small slam with 33 combined points, a grand slam with 37.

2. Bid a small slam directly if there is no danger of losing the first two tricks.

3. Blackwood four notrump asks for aces with step responses: five clubs — no ace, and so on. Use it when you have chosen a suit. Avoid it when you have a weak suit or a void suit.

4. When you have fixed a suit with a raise, make a cuebid in another suit to show control of that suit and slam interest.

5. When finessing, tend to finesse the lowest plausible card.

After a week of hard work you deserve some rest. All you are expected to do today is to answer questions reviewing what you have learned so far.

REVIEW QUESTIONS

1. How many high-card points must the partnership have in order to be sure that the opposition does not have an ace? If you have this total, what contract suggests itself?

2. If the opponents bid a game and you have 14 high-card points, how many do you expect your partner to have?

3. How many total points (high cards plus assets) do each of the following hands have? And would you open the bidding?

    a) ♠ Q 10 7 6 4 3   b) ♠ A Q 8 7 2
        ♡ 4   ♡ K J 6 5
        ◊ A K 8 2   ◊ 10 8 7 2
        ♣ Q 7   ♣ —

4. What do you know about your partner's hand if he opens one notrump?

5. What do you respond to one notrump with each of the following hands?

    a) ♠ K 8 4 3   b) ♠ 8 7 2   c) ♠ K 10 3
        ♡ J 4   ♡ Q 10 6   ♡ 7 6 2
        ◊ Q 6 5 3   ◊ J 2   ◊ A Q 9 8 2
        ♣ Q 9 7   ♣ A J 7 6 2   ♣ J 6

    d) ♠ A J 5   e) ♠ A J 5   f) ♠ A Q 5
        ♡ K Q 4   ♡ K Q 4   ♡ K Q 4
        ◊ Q J 3 2   ◊ A J 3 2   ◊ A Q J 2
        ♣ K 10 3   ♣ K 10 3   ♣ K J 2

g) ♠ 6 5 4 3 2   h) ♠ A J 5 4 3 2   i) ♠ A J 5 4 3
   ♡ 3 2   ♡ 3 2   ♡ 3 2
   ◇ 5 4 3 2   ◇ A 4 3 2   ◇ A 4 3 2
   ♣ 3 2   ♣ 2   ♣ J 2

j) ♠ A J 5 4 3
   ♡ A Q
   ◇ A J 3 2
   ♣ 3 2

6. Answer three questions about each of the following suit combinations: (i) How many tricks are you sure to make? (ii) What is the greatest number of tricks you can hope to make eventually? (iii) What will your first play be?

   You can lead from either hand and can afford to lose the lead. But play to save an entry if you will need one.

a) **Dummy**   b) **Dummy**   c) **Dummy**
   K J 10 9 8   A J 3 2   A J 4 3 2

   You   **You**   **You**
   Q   K 4   K 5

d) **Dummy**   e) **Dummy**   f) **Dummy**
   A 4 3 2   A K 5 4 3 2   K 5 4 3 2

   You   **You**   **You**
   K J   7 6   8 7 6

7. Listen to the opponents' bidding in each of the following situations and then answer three questions: (i) About how many points does the opener have? (ii) About how many points does the responder have? (iii) How many trumps do you expect each opponent to have?

a)
Opener	Responder
1♡	1NT
4♡	pass

b)
Opener	Responder
1♡	2♡
3◇	4♡

c)
Opener	Responder
1♡	3♡
pass	pass

d)
Opener	Responder
1♡	1♠
2♣	3♡
4♡	pass

e)
Opener	Responder
1♣	1♡
1♠	4♠
pass	

f)
Opener	Responder
1♣	1♡
2NT	3◇
3♡	4♡
pass	

g) Opener	Responder	h) Opener	Responder	i) Opener	Responder
1♦	1♠	1♣	1♠	1♦	2♠
3♣	3♠	2♡	4♡	3♦	3♠
4♠	pass	pass		3 NT	4♠
				pass	

8. What are the three common ways to head for a slam?

REVIEW ANSWERS

1. Thirty-seven out of a possible 40. The most the opponents can have is a king, and a grand slam contract should be available.

2. If they have 26, for their game bid, and you have 14, that accounts for all the 40 in the deck. That seems to leave your partner with zero, but he might have a little if the opponents are relying on some assets to count to 26.

3. (a) Eleven high-card points plus 1 asset for the spade length and 1 for the singleton heart: The total is 13, just enough to open.
   (b) Ten high-card points plus 1 asset for the spade length and 2 for the club void: the total is 13, just enough to open.

4. The one notrump bidder shows 15-17 points, but he may be counting one asset for a five-card suit. He also has a balanced hand: no more than one doubleton, and no singletons or voids.

5. (a) Pass. You are happy in notrump, but your 8 points cannot produce 26 even if your partner has a 17-point maximum.
   (b) Two notrump, inviting game. Opener passes with a minimum, or continues to three notrump with a maximum.
   (c) Three notrump. With 1 asset for the diamond length you can count 26. Notrump is the only game worth considering.
   (d) Four notrump, inviting six notrump. If your partner has 17 points the combined hands have 33. He continues with a maximum.
   (e) Six notrump: 33 points are guaranteed, and there cannot be the 37 needed for seven notrump.
   (f) Seven notrump: 37 points are guaranteed.

(g) Two spades[1], commanding partner to pass. You do not expect to make two spades, but you expect to do better than your partner would in one notrump. An eight-card fit is probable though not certain.

(h) Four spades[2]. You have 11 points, counting 2 assets, so the total is at least 26 and an eight-card fit is guaranteed.

(i) Three spades[3]. Your 1 asset gives you a 10-point total, so you can make a forcing jump in a new suit. This suggests a five-card suit, allowing partner to raise with three or four spades and revert to three notrump with a doubleton.

(j) Three spades[4], forcing. You are headed toward slam, with at least 32 points, including an asset, in the combined hands. But first you must find out whether there is an eight-card spade fit. Your partner's rebid will give you the answer.

6. (a) Four tricks are guaranteed, losing one trick to the ace. To save entries, play the king immediately, either leading it or leading the queen and overtaking. If you do not do this, an opponent can hold up his ace and make matters harder for you.

(b) Two tricks are guaranteed and there is a chance of a third. Start by playing the king and then lead the four. Unless the queen appears (most unlikely), finesse the jack in the hope that the queen is on your left. Playing the king and ace first might work, but is a poorer chance: if there are four cards on your left and three on your right, the queen is likely to be part of the four-card holding.

(c) Two tricks are guaranteed but you certainly expect to make more, perhaps even five. On a lucky day you will find that the player on your left has three cards including the queen. So start with the king (leading from either hand) and lead the five to finesse the jack. This can give you five tricks, but most of the time you will make three or four.

(d) Two tricks are sure, and there is a chance of three. Lead low from dummy and finesse the jack. If it wins you will have three tricks, and if not you still have two. Either way there will be a block, and you will need an entry to dummy to score the ace.

1, 2, 3, 4. Or use a transfer bid; see page 152.

(e) You have an excellent chance of making five tricks. On a very bad day, when one opponent has all five missing cards, you will make only three. You must lose one trick, so lose it at once, by a ducking play saving an entry to the dummy: lead a low card from one hand and play a low card from the other hand also. Then you will take the next five tricks if, as is likely, the opposing cards split three-two.

(f) No tricks are guaranteed: on a very bad day your right-hand opponent will have all five missing cards. You have a fair chance (about one in three) of making three tricks. You must hope that the opposing cards split three-two and that the ace is on your left. You need to duck a trick, and to lead from your hand towards the king in the dummy. It is slightly better to make the ducking play first, although that might not always be convenient.

7. (a) The one-notrump response showed 6-9 points and denied heart support. Responder has at most two hearts. The opener has about 20 points, since he can afford to insist on game opposite a weak hand. He thinks there is an eight-card fit, so he is likely (but not certain) to have seven hearts. Responder could have a singleton or even a void.

(b) The raise to two hearts showed 6-9 and at least three hearts. Three diamonds invited game, so the opener is likely to have 17-18. The responder accepted the invitation, so is likely to have 8-9. With 6-7 he would have signed off in three hearts. The trump fit is at least five-three and may be better.

(c) The three-heart jump raise showed four-card support and about 11 points. This is a strong invitation to game, so the opener must have a minimum, probably just 13 points. The trump fit is probably five-four but might be better.

(d) Delayed support for a major suit usually shows exactly three cards. Jumps by responder are usually invitations to game, so he must have about 11 points. The opener would pass with a minimum hand, so he is likely to have 15-18 points. The fit is likely to be five-three but might be six-three.

(e) The opener may have a good deal more than a minimum. He is probably in the 13-17 range. The responder has enough to insist on game, probably 13-16. The trump fit is almost certain to be four-four.

(f) The opener's two-notrump rebid showed 18-20. His delayed support for hearts showed three, and the fit is probably five-three. The responder's strength is uncertain: probably 6-11.

(g) The opener's new-suit jump rebid showed a monster hand. He guaranteed game opposite a possible 6 points, so he must have about 20. Responder probably has 6-10 points, and the fit is likely to be six-two.

(h) Since the opener pushed the bidding up, past two of his first suit, he has reversed, showing 17-18 points. Responder probably has 8-12, and the heart fit is likely to be four-four.

(i) The jump-shift response of two spades showed at least 17 points and slam interest. Responder does not have much more or he would have bid more. The opener has a minimum, about 13 points, and the trump fit, since responder has insisted on spades in the face of discouragement, is probably seven-one or seven-zero.

8. The first is direct bidding: bid the slam, or invite by bidding the agreed major suit at the five-level. The second is Blackwood, checking aces with four notrump when that is the only problem. The third is the cuebid: when the suit is agreed, bid another suit to show control and imply weakness elsewhere.

One significant word must now be introduced: **vulnerability**.

In the original form of contract bridge, devised by Harold Vanderbilt in 1925, the unit of play was a **rubber**, with a large bonus for the first pair to win two games. When you had won your first game you became **vulnerable**, and the penalties for failure increased.

Rubber bridge is now rarely played in North America, but in all forms of the game circumstances will dictate whether you are vulnerable (see pages 218-219).

In the first eight lessons vulnerability was not mentioned because it is not important when one partnership is in full charge of the auction. But it is a significant factor when both partnerships are involved in the bidding, directly or potentially.

A vulnerable penalty is almost twice as great as a nonvulnerable penalty. So a player who is vulnerable must bid more cautiously if there is a real danger of being doubled by an opponent. The danger is trivial when the opponents are silent, but serious if they begin the bidding. So if an opponent starts the proceedings and you take action you will be very aware of the vulnerability, and so will the other three players.

Suppose you have this hand:

♠ 4 3   ♡ K Q 9 8 3   ◇ A J 4 2   ♣ K 2

If you were the dealer you would certainly bid one heart. If an opponent opens the bidding you are inclined to bid hearts (you are making an **overcall**), but you must look at the circumstances: the vulnerability and the level.

The risk of bidding is a maximum if you are vulnerable and have to bid at the two-level. So if an opponent opens one spade and you are vulnerable, discretion dictates a pass. Add one more heart, giving you a six-card suit, and two hearts would be appropriate. Not vulnerable you could venture two hearts with the hand shown, and a one heart overcall would be right at any vulnerability if the opening bid were one club.

The safest time to overcall is at the one-level, not vulnerable. Take the diamond ace away from the above hand, and one heart is still an acceptable overcall of one club if you are not vulnerable.

All overcalls are based on a five-card or longer suit, and the quality of the suit is important: lean toward bidding if the suit is strong, and toward passing if the suit is weak. Most overcalls are in the 13-16-point range, and therefore equivalent to a minimum opening bid.

The following table is worth noting:

Level	Not Vulnerable	Vulnerable
One-level	Be aggressive	Normal
Two-level	Normal	Be cautious

Bearing this in mind, try to answer the following question. It is only fair to warn you that your answer is sure to be wrong. The bidding has started:

West	North	East	South
Dealer	Partner	Opponent	You
1♣	1♠	pass	??

Your hand is:

♠ K74   ♡ A843   ◇ AJ86   ♣ J6

What do you bid?

If your partner had opened the bidding with one spade, you could have marked time with two diamonds, showing at least 10 points and asking for a description. But when, as here, partner has overcalled the situation is quite different. The guideline is: *if the opponents open, almost any bid is natural and non-forcing.*

So if you bid two diamonds (or two hearts) your partner will think that you dislike his suit and have a long, strong suit of your own.

You know that your partner has at least five spades for his overcall, so a normal fit is guaranteed. You can certainly play a spade contract, but is there a game?

If you chose to bid two spades you were much too cautious. How about three spades? Or four spades?

Either of those bids can be wrong — or perhaps right.

Instead of selecting a bid, you should have asked a question: who is vulnerable?

To repeat: if both sides are bidding, it is vital to keep an eye on the vulnerability.

Suppose that you are vulnerable. In that case your partner should have an opening bid as well as a five-card suit. You can see 26 points in the combined hands, so you can bid four spades.

If you are not vulnerable, your partner may have less than an opening bid for his overcall. You must allow for the possibility that he has only about 10 points so your bid should be invitational: three spades. Partner will pass if he has a moth-eaten overcall, but will continue if he has the values for an opening bid.

The moral is that you must take the opposite tack to your partner. If he is being aggressive, because you are not vulnerable, you must be cautious. If he is being cautious, because you are vulnerable, you must be aggressive. So: *not vulnerable, overcall aggressively, raise cautiously; vulnerable, overcall cautiously, raise aggressively.*

All this relates to simple suit overcalls at the minimum level. However, there are three other types of overcalls to note.

Higher overcalls. Overcalls that skip one or more levels (one diamond-two spades, or one diamond-three spades) are in principle weak. They show long, strong suits, with at least six cards and usually more, and follow the rules for **preemptive bids** set out on page 173. The vulnerability is again a factor: be aggressive when not vulnerable, and cautious when vulnerable.

However, the traditional meaning of a single jump (one diamond-two spades, or one spade-three diamonds) is different. It shows a strong six-card suit and a hand slightly too good for a normal overcall. The point count is likely to be about 17. Whether you play modern weak jump overcalls or traditional strong jump overcalls is something to discuss with a new partner.

One notrump overcall. If your right-hand opponent bids a suit and you overcall one notrump, you show a hand worth slightly better than a one-notrump opening (roughly 16-18 points) and a **stopper**, or **guard**, in the enemy suit. A stopper is a high card with which you expect to take an early trick in the opponents' suit if they lead it. Partner responds as he would to a one-notrump opening, but can also bid the enemy suit as a probe for more information.

Two notrump overcall. This is an artificial bid, or convention. It shows two suits, the low-ranking ones, and the values, allowing for vulnerability, for a normal overcall. So over one spade (or one heart), two notrump shows at least five clubs and at least five diamonds. If the opening bid was a minor suit, the two notrump overcall shows the other minor suit and hearts. This **Unusual Notrump** bid, which can apply in some other situations when a natural meaning is improbable, hardly ever shows spades.

Now it is time to play. You are North, and your hand is:

♠ K J 6 2   ♡ Q 5 3   ◇ 7   ♣ K J 10 8 4

The bidding is:

West	North	East	South
	You		Partner
		1◇	1♠
2◇	??		

What do you bid?

I hope I did not catch you again in this small trap. *You should be demanding to know the vulnerability.*

Both sides are vulnerable. Now what do you bid?

Answer: Four spades.

Your partner's vulnerable overcall showed at least a five-card suit and a hand that would have opened the bidding — that is, 13 points. You know there is a nine-card fit, so your 2 assets have doubled. You can count to 27 and should bid game. If your partner had overcalled not vulnerable, he might have only about 10 points and you would have to be content with a cautious invitation of three spades.

Remember that unless you are making a forcing bid you must bid the full value of your hand.

If you can count the values for game, do not give your partner a chance to stop below game.

Now move round the table and play the hand for your partner. You see this:

NORTH

♠ K J 6 2
♡ Q 5 3
◇ 7
♣ K J 10 8 4

West leads the
diamond queen

SOUTH

♠ A 10 9 7 3
♡ K 8 4
◇ 9 2
♣ A Q 3

At first glance you seem to be in very good shape. There are only two sure losers, one in each red suit. But take a closer look, and consider what might go wrong.

The situation in the trump suit is called a **two-way finesse**. Since there are only four spades missing, there are three acceptable ways to play the suit:

1. Play the ace and king and hope the queen falls.

2. Play the ace and run the ten, winning if West has the queen, losing if East has the queen.

3. Play the king and lead to the ten, winning if East has the queen and losing if West has the queen.

There is little to choose among the three plays, and circumstances will usually dictate which one is right in a particular instance. That will be the case here, as we shall see.

In hearts we are sure to lose the ace and we are in danger of losing another trick too. Our plan is to discard a heart on dummy's clubs, but we cannot do that until trumps have been drawn.

In diamonds we have one obvious loser, and the second round can be ruffed in the dummy. Clubs are fully controlled, but we cannot lead them until we have drawn the enemy trumps.

Do we plan to draw trumps? Yes. Since we have plenty of trumps in the dummy, the diamond ruff can wait.

To start with, the opponents are in charge. West wins the first trick with the diamond queen and shifts to the heart jack. What do you play from the dummy?

Answer: a low heart.

If you play the queen East will take the ace and continue the suit, leaving you in trouble. In general you should save your honor cards for a rainy day rather than present them for slaughter.

If East puts up his ace of hearts he makes life easy for you. But he is not on your side, and plays low. Quite rightly, he preserves his ace in the hope that it will eventually capture dummy's queen. That is a general objective for both sides: when possible, make sure your high cards capture enemy high cards.

You win with the queen and face the moment of truth in this position:

NORTH

♠ K J 6 2

♡ Q 5

♢ —

♣ K J 10 8 4

SOUTH

♠ A 10 9 7 3

♡ 8 4

♢ 9

♣ A Q 3

You are, of course, certain that the ace of hearts is on your right. Remember that East opened the bidding and therefore was looking at 13 points.

What is the danger? Obviously, that West will gain the lead and play another heart. If you can prevent that happening you are safe.

Now connect that thought with your problem in the trump suit. You know you may have to lose a trump trick, but it will not matter if you lose it to East. If he gains the lead he cannot hurt you in hearts.

The right way to play trumps is therefore plan (2) above: play the ace, follow with the ten, and finesse. If West has the queen it is trapped. If East has it he will make a trick, but you are safe.

As it happens this play gives you an extra trick because the whole hand was as shown below (the dealer was East and both sides were vulnerable).

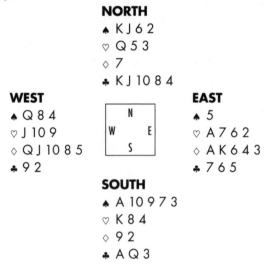

NORTH
♠ K J 6 2
♡ Q 5 3
◊ 7
♣ K J 10 8 4

WEST
♠ Q 8 4
♡ J 10 9
◊ Q J 10 8 5
♣ 9 2

EAST
♠ 5
♡ A 7 6 2
◊ A K 6 4 3
♣ 7 6 5

SOUTH
♠ A 10 9 7 3
♡ K 8 4
◊ 9 2
♣ A Q 3

Notice that any other plan of play would have failed. Playing the top spades and then leading clubs would have allowed West to ruff and lead a heart before any discards could be made from the South hand.

There are some guidelines about opening leads that need to be understood.

The most desirable lead is from touching high cards. The lead of a high card usually shows that the player has the card ranking immediately below and denies the card immediately above. So West's lead of the queen of diamonds promised the jack but denied the king.

However, the lead of a king[1] is an exception. It can be supported by the queen or the ace. If East were on lead on this deal he would choose the king of diamonds.

---

1. Many modern players lead the ace from an ace-king combination; discuss this with a new partner.

The choice of opening lead is a complicated matter on which experts often disagree. But other things being equal one should tend to follow this order:

1. *Good leads.* The honor sequence, with two or more touching high cards. Against a notrump contract a little stiffening is needed: queen from queen-jack-nine-two but two from queen-jack-three-two.

2. *Neutral leads.* Worthless suits of any length. May not do much good, but seldom do any harm.

3. *Bad leads.* Broken suits, with one or two high cards not in sequence. These often help the enemy.

Once the suit has been chosen, the actual card to lead is easier. This is the order of preference when touching honors are not available:

1. Fourth card from length: queen-eight-five-*two*; king-jack-seven-*three*-two.

2. Third card from three: king-six-*four*.

3. Top card of two: *queen*-four; *eight*-four.

Never lead the fifth card, or one below it. Virtually never lead the second card. (King-*jack*-ten is an exception, and some players avoid that.)

A few special points:

- Tend to lead long suits, even broken ones, against notrump, but tend toward a safe lead, from worthless suits, at a trump contract.

- Tend to lead a suit your partner has bid at any contract.

- Tend to avoid leading a suit an opponent has bid — particularly your right-hand opponent.

- A singleton lead is usually good against a trump contract, bad against notrump.

- Against a trump contract never lead low from a suit headed by the ace.

- Consider a trump lead with two or three small cards, but not with a singleton. Against notrump, tend to lead a major rather than a minor.

1. If your right-hand opponent (who is not vulnerable) has opened one heart, decide what you would bid with each of the following hands (i) not vulnerable, and (ii) vulnerable.

   a) ♠ K 9 8 7 2
      ♡ 9 6 2
      ◇ A Q
      ♣ 7 5 4

   b) ♠ 7 5 4
      ♡ 9 6 2
      ◇ A Q
      ♣ A K 10 8 6

2. If your left-hand opponent (who is not vulnerable) opens one heart and your partner overcalls one spade, what should you bid with each of the following hands (i) not vulnerable, and (ii) vulnerable?

   a) ♠ A 10 3
      ♡ 8 5 4
      ◇ J 6
      ♣ K Q 9 6 4

   b) ♠ A 10 3
      ♡ 8 5 4
      ◇ K 6
      ♣ K Q 9 6 4

3. If your opponents bid one notrump-three notrump what would you lead with each of the following hands?

   a) ♠ A Q 8 4 3
      ♡ K Q J
      ◇ 5 2
      ♣ 7 6 2

   b) ♠ K Q J 4
      ♡ Q 8 6 3 2
      ◇ 10 7 2
      ♣ 5

   c) ♠ 8 6 2
      ♡ Q 6 2
      ◇ 10 7 4 3
      ♣ A 7 2

QUIZ ANSWERS

1. (a) If you are not vulnerable, one spade is appropriate. But you must pass if vulnerable, for an overcall would show the values for an opening bid.

   (b) You have opening-bid values, and can certainly bid two clubs if not vulnerable. Vulnerable at the two-level the bid would be risky, so pass. A sixth club would be needed for that action.

2. (a) Not vulnerable, a raise to two spades is enough. At the one-level, not vulnerable, partner may have made an aggressive overcall with about 10 points. Vulnerable, you can assume an opening bid and invite with three spades. Partner must have at least a five-card suit, so a normal fit is guaranteed.

(b) Not vulnerable, raise to three spades, inviting game. You must allow for the chance that partner has overcalled with about 10 points. But vulnerable you can bid four spades, expecting your partner to have the values for an opening bid.

3. (a) The spade four, fourth-best from the long suit. If your partner gains the lead and returns spades there is a good chance that you will take four tricks in the suit. (In a suit contract you would lead the heart king, giving nothing away.)

(b) Normally the longest suit should be chosen, and it might be right to lead the heart three (fourth from the top, remember). But the spade suit is so much stronger than the hearts that the spade king is the right choice.

(c) There is no clear lead, but a spade is indicated. When in doubt against notrump prefer a major to a minor, because the opponents will often have a concealed minor suit. A spade is less likely to give away a trick than a heart. Which spade to lead, with three small cards, is a matter of style. Some players lead high, some low, and a few middle.

ESSENTIALS TO REMEMBER

1. Overcalls guarantee at least a five-card suit and about the values for a minimum opening; a little less is possible not vulnerable at the one-level. A little more is needed vulnerable at the two-level, which is normally done on a six-card suit.

2. Always raise the overcall with three-card support or better: cautiously not vulnerable, aggressively vulnerable.

3. Jump overcalls to any level show long, strong suits but weak hands. One notrump overcalls are roughly equivalent to a notrump opening bid. Two notrump jump overcalls are Unusual, showing at least five cards in each of the low-ranking unbid suits.

4. High-card leads show the next-ranking card (except king from ace-king).

5. Against notrump lead a promising long suit, usually a major.

6. Against a suit, tend to lead safely.

7. Lead the fourth card from length; the third from three; the top of two.

8. Lead partner's suit but not an opponent's suit.

In the early days of bridge it was realized that when an opponent
opens the bidding in a suit a double has no useful natural meaning.
So it was given a very important artificial use: *a double of an opening*
suit bid shows opening values and asks partner to choose a suit[1].

Take out double

West	North	East	South
	Partner	Opener	You
		1◊	dbl

This is called a **takeout double**, because partner is asked to take it
out. Typically, the doubler will have at least three cards in each unbid
suit. This might be your hand on the auction shown:

♠ A Q 6 3   ♡ K J 5 2   ◊ 7 6   ♣ K 8 4

The point count is likely to be 13-16, but a variety of stronger
hands are possible. If, for example, you hold about 18 points and a
five-card suit, you are too strong for a normal overcall. A takeout
double followed by a bid of the suit is the way to go. With strong
hands the requirement to have three cards in each unbid suit does
not apply.

Notice that the double would be quite wrong with the hand
shown after an opening bid of one spade or one heart. The shortage
in diamonds would be a deterrent, since partner might pick that suit.
With this hand, you would have to pass an opening bid of one heart
or one spade. (Passing is usually the right action with length and
strength in the opponent's suit, even with a strong hand.)

---

1. Note that we are talking only of opening suit bids. Doubles of notrump
   bids are always for penalties.

The takeout double shown above presents the doubler's partner with a wide variety of options. The most important, assuming a one-diamond opening, are the following.

1. One heart, one spade, or two clubs. Minimum suit bids show little or nothing, 0-8 points, obeying partner's command to pick a suit. Bid your longest suit (but not the opponent's suit!), and in emergency a three-card suit.

2. Two hearts, two spades, and three clubs. Jump suit bids invite game with 9-11 points and usually a five-card suit.

3. Four spades, four hearts. Usually a six-card or longer suit, combined 26 points.

4. One notrump (6-9), two notrump (10-12) and three no-trump (13-16) promise some strength in the enemy suit and deny interest in a major-suit game.

5. Pass. Very rare, showing great length and strength in the enemy suit. This action does not show weakness, but the expectation of a penalty.

Remember the general principle we have stated already: *if the opponents open the bidding, normal bids are never forcing.* What constitutes an abnormal bid? Consider this problem:

♠ K J 6 2   ♡ A Q 5 3   ◇ 7 4 2   ♣ Q J

West	North	East	South
Opener	Partner		You
1◇	dbl	pass	??

You are looking at a 13-point opening bid, and West and North also have opening values. This adds up to 39 points, perhaps including a few assets, and there are only 40 points in the deck. The unfortunate East is virtually destitute: he may well have a **yarborough**, a hand with no card higher than a nine.

Your partner cannot have the strong type of double, with 17 points or more, for there would then be more than 40 points in the deck. You can be sure that he has about 13 points, and he is likely to have three or four cards in each major suit.

You know a great deal, but you still do not know what to do. You want to play in four spades or four hearts, and it is highly probable that there is a normal fit in at least one of them. But if you just take a stab at four spades that may turn out to be a four-three fit, a bad stab. Similarly, four hearts can be the wrong choice.

The solution is to do something wildly improbable that will astonish your partner: *bid two diamonds.*

Diamonds is the opponent's suit, and it is impossible that you would wish to play there. In the very unlikely event that you held long, strong diamonds you would pass the double for penalties.

Two diamonds has no natural meaning, but it has a useful artificial meaning: I think we have a game. It implies doubt about the right game, and asks the doubler to describe his hand. It is highly probable that partner will bid two spades or two hearts, and the normal fit will have been found.

Two diamonds is another form of cuebid. A bid in the opponents' suit below game, in many situations, has no relation to the enemy suit: it simply suggests a search for the best available game.

Now let's play. The player on your left deals and bids one club. Your partner doubles for takeout, the next player passes, and you are looking at:

♠ A K J 10 4   ♡ 8 4   ◇ 9 5 4   ♣ J 7 3

West	North	East	South
	Partner		You
1♣	dbl	pass	??

You are not strong enough to insist on game by bidding four spades, but you are much too strong to bid one spade. That bid, remember, would have to be made even if you had no points at all. The intermediate course is to jump to two spades, inviting game. This shows about 10 points. A normal fit is virtually guaranteed, so your long-suit asset is valid.

Your jump asks partner to continue with a little extra. His extra is very little indeed, but he shows his confidence in your playing skill by bidding four spades. The king of clubs is led and you see this:

NORTH
♠ Q 8 7 3
♡ A Q J
◊ A J 10 8
♣ 10 6

West leads the club king

SOUTH
♠ A K J 10 4
♡ 8 4
◊ 9 5 4
♣ J 7 3

In your preliminary survey, before touching a card, you note that you are in full control of the trump suit. You will lose two club tricks, and you can eventually ruff a club in dummy. You will surely lose one trick in diamonds. There is some danger of losing another diamond trick, and there is a possible heart loser.

Some finessing will be called for in the red suits. The good news is that West opened the bidding. He must have 13 points, of some kind, which does not leave much for East.

West leads the king of clubs followed by the ace and the queen. Obviously you will ruff in the dummy, but what with?

The safe thing to do is to ruff with the queen, a card you can well spare since the high trumps in your hand leave you in full control of the suit. The unsafe play is to ruff low, running an unnecessary risk that East will be able to overruff by playing a higher trump than dummy.

There is a strong indication that a careless ruff with a low trump would get its just deserts in the form of an overruff. East played the eight and two of clubs on the first two tricks, which as we shall see later asks West to play another club. He is surely poised for an overruff.

When you ruff with the spade queen East discards a heart, thwarted in his plan to overruff the dummy. You work on trumps, playing the ace and king, and find that the opponents produce two each. That takes care of that, and it is time to try a red suit, leading low to high.

Which red suit?

You could lead a heart, aiming to finesse the jack or queen in the hope that West has the king. But that is putting all your eggs in the heart basket. If it loses you are dead: there is no way to escape losing a diamond trick.

Rather than pin your hopes on a fifty-fifty chance, you should lead diamonds. If West has the king of diamonds, or the queen of diamonds, or both, you can score three diamond tricks. Eventually you can discard a heart from your hand and avoid the heart finesse altogether.

Carrying out this plan, you lead a diamond. West plays low, you play the ten (or jack) from dummy, and East wins with the queen. East does not have any black cards, so he gives you some help by returning a heart. Dummy's jack wins.

You are now in the wrong hand to lead a red suit. To enter your hand you play dummy's last trump and win with the jack. The position is now this:

NORTH

♠ —
♡ A Q
◇ A J 8
♣ —

SOUTH

♠ 10 4
♡ 8
◇ 9 5
♣ —

There is still a finessing choice available. A successful heart finesse will provide a diamond discard, and vice versa.

It is generally wrong to change plans in midstream. Your idea was to work on diamonds, and you should persevere with that. You play the diamond nine[2], and when the king appears from West you can

---

2. Note for advanced players only: the final decision is based on a principle called **restricted choice**. With both the king and queen of diamonds East might have won the first diamond trick with the king.

save time by claiming the remaining tricks.

The complete deal was:

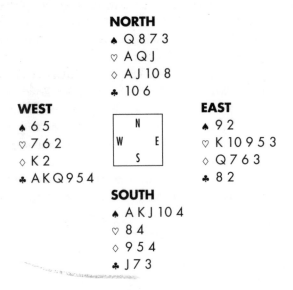

NORTH
- ♠ Q 8 7 3
- ♡ A Q J
- ◇ A J 10 8
- ♣ 10 6

WEST
- ♠ 6 5
- ♡ 7 6 2
- ◇ K 2
- ♣ A K Q 9 5 4

EAST
- ♠ 9 2
- ♡ K 10 9 5 3
- ◇ Q 7 6 3
- ♣ 8 2

SOUTH
- ♠ A K J 10 4
- ♡ 8 4
- ◇ 9 5 4
- ♣ J 7 3

HIGH-LOW SIGNAL

East's play in clubs on the deal above is an example of the commonest **signal** used by defenders, the high-low to encourage the play of a suit.

It may be used on the first trick when partner leads an honor:

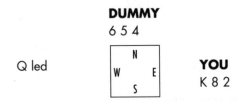

DUMMY
6 5 4

Q led

YOU
K 8 2

Play the eight, encouraging partner to continue by showing that you have a useful honor card. Your partner has to have the jack, and you want to tell him to continue. If you played the two your play would be discouraging, telling partner that you have no help in the suit. If you held ten-eight-two, the eight would again be the right play, showing that you have a useful card.

Another situation occurs in a suit contract. Suppose we are in four spades:

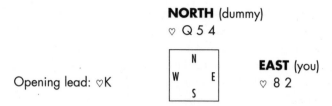

NORTH (dummy)
♡ Q 5 4

Opening lead: ♡K

EAST (you)
♡ 8 2

You play the eight, followed by the two. This encourages partner to continue, and you can ruff the third round.

Another important use of this signal is in discarding. Throw a high card to advise partner that you want him to lead a suit. And always signal as loudly as possible. If you are going to signal holding king-queen-jack-ten, throw the king. Any signal from an honor sequence like this denies the card above.

There are two other important signals. They apply when you cannot want your partner to play the suit in which the signal is given.

COUNT SIGNAL

If dummy has a long, strong suit it can be vital to give partner a message:

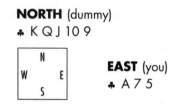

NORTH (dummy)
♣ K Q J 10 9

EAST (you)
♣ A 7 5

The contract is three notrump. Dummy has the strong club suit shown but not much else. The decision you have to make is: when do you take your ace? We have said already that you should not be in a hurry to take a sure trick in the opponents' suit. But the exact timing is vital.

If you take your ace too early you will leave South with a way to reach the dummy. If you take it too late you give him a trick he could not otherwise make.

Your aim should be to put your ace on South's last card. If he has two cards you should take the second trick, and so on. But how do you know?

Your partner tells you with a **count signal**: *high shows an even number of cards, low an odd number.* (A memory aid: high and even are four-letter words; low and odd are three-letter words.)

If your partner plays the two of clubs on the first round of the suit, a low card, you assume he has three cards. That leaves South with two, so refuse the first club trick and win the second. If your partner plays the eight, a high card, you know he cannot have three cards. The bidding will also usually give you a clue. If you think your partner has two cards then South has three and you hold up your ace until the third round.

This count signal applies whenever dummy has some length and strength. Like all signals, it needs cooperation: one partner sends, and one partner decodes.

SUIT-PREFERENCE SIGNAL

Another important signal is made when you are trying to direct your partner's attention to a completely different suit.

Suppose you are defending four spades and lead the ace of diamonds. Your partner discards, so that you know he can ruff the next diamond lead.

The spot card you choose can tell him which suit to return after he ruffs the next diamond. A low diamond would ask for the low-ranking club suit. A high diamond would ask for the high-ranking heart suit.

QUIZ

1. If the player on your right bids one club, both sides vulnerable, what would you bid with each of the following hands?

a)	b)	c)
♠ K 5 4	♠ A Q 8 7 2	♠ A Q 8 7
♡ A Q 6 3	♡ A 8 2	♡ K J 6 3
◇ K J 9 4 2	◇ K Q 6	◇ 4
♣ 6	♣ K 5	♣ A 9 8 4

2. Both sides are vulnerable. What would you bid with each of the following hands after the bidding shown?

West	North	East	South
1♣	dbl	pass	??

a) ♠ 5 4 3 2
♡ 4 3 2
◊ 4 3 2
♣ 4 3 2

b) ♠ K J 9 7 5 4
♡ A 6 2
◊ K 4
♣ 8 2

c) ♠ K 9 7 5 4
♡ A 6 2
◊ K 2
♣ 8 3 2

d) ♠ Q 4
♡ K J 5
◊ 10 8 7 2
♣ A J 8 3

e) ♠ K 4
♡ 8 2
◊ J 8 3
♣ Q J 10 8 6 2

f) ♠ K 9 4 2
♡ K 9 4 2
◊ A
♣ K 7 6 2

3. Suppose that you are defending four spades, and when trumps are led your partner discards the club queen. Dummy is on your left and has three small clubs.

    (a) What do you think your partner has in clubs?
    (b) If you have the king what will you do about it?
    (c) If you have the ace what will you do about it?

QUIZ	ANSWERS

1. (a) Double, for takeout, of course. Showing opening values with support for the unbid suits gives a much better picture of your hand than an overcall in diamonds, which would put all your eggs in that basket.
    (b) Double. With 18 high-card points you are too strong to over-call one spade. That bid is rarely made with more than 16 points. A double followed by a spade bid will show a hand that was too strong to overcall.
    (c) Pass. This would be an ideal hand for a double of one dia-mond, but you cannot double one club because your partner would expect you to have at least three diamonds. You cannot bid one spade or one heart because an overcall promises a

five-card suit. You have to pass. This is often necessary with a good hand, sometimes much better than this one, with length in the enemy suit.

2. (a) One spade. Your partner has ordered you to bid, and you must obey orders. One spade does not promise any points at all, and your partner knows that. The problem would be harder if one of the spades were a club. In that case one diamond, even with only three cards, would be the least of evils. In real life, however, this particular misfortune will never face you: if you are very weak the player on your right can be expected to do something, and you will be relieved of the obligation to bid.

    (b) Four spades. You can assume that partner has three spades, so you have a nine-card fit and your 1 asset doubles. You think you can make game in spades, so bid it.

    (c) Two spades. Not quite enough to insist on game, so invite by jumping to two spades. One spade would be feeble, leaving partner with the impression of a very weak hand.

    (d) Two notrump. A strong invitation to game in notrump, suggesting 10-12 high-card points. You have the enemy club suit well protected, and no reason to think that there is a normal fit in a major suit.

    (e) Pass. The rare situation in which you pass for penalties, expecting to kill the opponents in one club. If they retreat into another suit your partner is likely to be able to double that.

    (f) Two clubs. This is a cuebid, announcing that you expect to make a game but are not sure where. This is the only way to make your partner bid. He knows that you cannot want to play in the opponent's club suit.

3. (a) Before throwing the queen partner probably had queen-jack-ten-nine or ace-queen-jack-ten. He has promised the jack and denied the king.

    (b) Lead clubs if you get the chance. It cannot hurt you and may help.

    (c) Avoid leading clubs. The king is on your right, and you want to capture it with your ace. Wait for someone else to lead clubs.

ESSENTIALS TO REMEMBER

1. A typical takeout double of an enemy suit bid shows 13-16 points and at least three cards in each unbid suit. Stronger hands are possible, with almost any distribution. There is no upper limit.

2. In response to a takeout double, bid as much as you can afford, preferably in a major suit. A pass shows length and strength in their suit. If you are looking for game and are not sure where, try a cuebid in their suit.

3. Play an unnecessarily high card, followed by a low card, to show a desire for partner to play the suit. This can be done in a suit partner has led, or when discarding.

4. Signal count in dummy's strong suit: high with an even number, low with odd.

5. In other circumstances the play of a high card can ask for a high-ranking suit, and the play of a low card can ask for a low-ranking suit.

Yesterday we studied in depth the commonest variety of takeout double, following an opposing bid of one of a suit. But doubles are made in a wide variety of other situations. Some of them are for takeout but most are for penalties, indicating an expectation of defeating the opponents' contract and making them pay a heavy price for bidding.

A sure recipe for bidding disaster is for your partner to think that your takeout double is for penalty or vice-versa. You must know how to classify doubles, putting them in the right category. The rule (remembering that a pass is not a bid) is this: *if the doubler's partner has not bid, a double of a low-level suit bid is for takeout.* All other doubles are for penalties. (Note: two exceptions will be noted on pages 215 and 216.)

Consider these three examples:

a)

West	North	East	South
	(partner)		(you)
			1♡
1NT	dbl		

b)

West	North	East	South
	(partner)		(you)
			pass
4♠	dbl		

c)

West	North	East	South
	(partner)		(you)
			1♣
1♡	pass	pass	dbl

In (a) your partner's double is for penalties for two reasons: it is a double of notrump, not a suit bid, and you have already made a bid. In (b) the double is also for penalties, because it is at the game level. A double of a partscore bid would be for takeout.

But the double in (c) is for takeout. The bid doubled is a partscore in a suit, and the doubler's partner has not bid. That the doubler has bid before is not a factor.

Of course it is not enough to know what the double means. What are the circumstances that call for a double?

Almost any double you make below the game level shows that you believe, or have reason to hope, that your partnership has most of the high-card strength: say, 21 or more out of the 40.

A normal takeout double shows that, like your opponent, you have opening values. In other situations the strength needed might be more or less, depending on circumstances.

In example (c) above you must have a very strong hand with at least 17 points. You have already shown 13 with your opening bid, and your partner could not scrape up a bid over one heart. He probably has fewer than 6 points, so you need 17 to have a fair prospect of 21 in the combined hands.

Suppose you are West with this hand:

♠ Q 8 7 2　♡ 6　♢ A 10 6 3　♣ K 10 5 4

West	North	East	South
			1NT
pass	2♡	pass	pass
??			

South has about 16 points and a balanced hand. North has at least five hearts and a weak hand: fewer than 8 high-card points. It is not clear whether you have most of the high cards, but you should nevertheless double for takeout. Your partner certainly has some high-card strength, since the opponents were not interested in game, and you have a good fit for any suit he picks.

Reopening the bidding when the opponents have stopped at a low level is called **balancing**. Be aggressive. *Tend to make a takeout double when short in the enemy suit.*

And, conversely, tend to pass when you have length in the enemy suit. If you held the hand shown above and the opponent bid two spades instead of two hearts, you would certainly pass.

For a low-level penalty double, shortage is also the key factor: tend to make a penalty double when short in partner's suit.

The hand shown above would be an ideal penalty double[1] if your partner opened one heart and the next player overcalled two clubs or two diamonds. But if the opening bid were one spade a double would be quite wrong: a raise to three spades would be indicated.

Now it is time to play. With both sides vulnerable you pick up as West:

♠ Q   ♡ K J 9 6 2   ◇ 8 7 5 2   ♣ A 10 3

West	North	East	South
(you)		(partner)	
		1♠	2♡
??			

This is the ideal moment to say 'double', for penalties. You have length and strength in the enemy suit, shortage in your partner's suit, and enough high cards to be confident that your partnership has most of the high-card strength.

Doubling two hearts, or any higher contract, runs a risk: if the opponents make their contract the double gives them a game[2]. But here the risk is negligible. The only question is how big the penalty will be.

Everyone passes and we lead the spade queen. We now see:

NORTH
♠ 7 6 4 2
♡ 5 4
◇ Q 9 4
♣ J 9 8 4

WEST
♠ Q
♡ K J 9 6 2
◇ 8 7 5 2
♣ A 10 3

```
        N
  W         E
        S
```

---

1. But see also page 129 for a modern use of this bid.
2. See scoring information on page 218.

Dummy plays low and East takes the ace. This play denies the king: it is normal to play as cheaply as possible on defense when you have equal cards (that is, two or more cards in sequence) and someone else leads the suit.

You expect your partner to return a spade so that you can ruff. Instead he plays the king of diamonds, winning the second trick, and then plays the spade jack. South covers with the king and you ruff.

Your partner's thoughtful play of the diamond king showed you that he has the ace. So you return that suit and dummy plays low. Your partner wins with the jack and takes the diamond ace. He follows with the spade ten, winning a trick as you discard a small club.

When your partner plays the spade nine South ruffs low and you overruff with the heart six. You lead your last diamond, and dummy ruffs. Your partner overruffs with the heart seven and South overruffs in his turn with the heart eight.

Your partnership already has seven tricks and South is still in trouble. The end-position is:

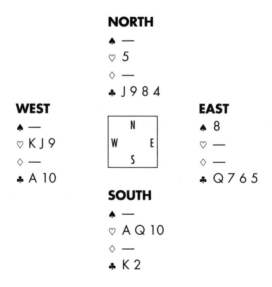

NORTH
♠ —
♡ 5
♢ —
♣ J 9 8 4

WEST
♠ —
♡ K J 9
♢ —
♣ A 10

EAST
♠ 8
♡ —
♢ —
♣ Q 7 6 5

SOUTH
♠ —
♡ A Q 10
♢ —
♣ K 2

South does something clever now. He leads the heart ten (or the queen) for an **endplay** against you. You win and must give him a trick, either by returning a trump or by leading the ace and another club. But either way you take three of the last five tricks and the contract is down five.

As we shall see later (p. 218) your score is 1400, more than twice what you would have scored if you had bid and made three notrump.

The complete deal was:

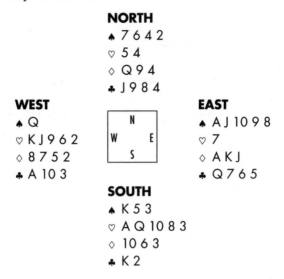

NORTH
♠ 7 6 4 2
♡ 5 4
◇ Q 9 4
♣ J 9 8 4

WEST
♠ Q
♡ K J 9 6 2
◇ 8 7 5 2
♣ A 10 3

EAST
♠ A J 10 9 8
♡ 7
◇ A K J
♣ Q 7 6 5

SOUTH
♠ K 5 3
♡ A Q 10 8 3
◇ 10 6 3
♣ K 2

You will note that in losing 1400 points South got his just deserts. As we discussed earlier (page 85), he was in the worst position to make an overcall, vulnerable at the two-level. He would have been in order, but only just, with an extra heart in his hand.

East's play of the spade ace on the first trick demonstrates simply two important principles of defensive play: *with equal cards, lead high, play low.*

This guideline is to help partner. By playing the ace, East denied possession of the king. By returning the jack later he promised the ten just as he would have done when making an original lead. Consider this suit layout:

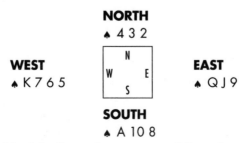

NORTH
♠ 4 3 2

WEST
♠ K 7 6 5

EAST
♠ Q J 9

SOUTH
♠ A 10 8

You (West) lead the five and your partner follows the rule by playing the jack, the lower of his equal cards. South wins with the ace and you now know that your partner has the queen: South would have won the trick with that card if he had held it. So it is safe for you to continue the suit when you regain the lead.

But if East had played the queen he would have denied the jack. Then you would know that South held that card, and continuing the suit would be risky.

A second principle to remember is: *third hand plays high, but...*

For two centuries, at bridge's forerunner, whist, players learned this rule. The third player should do his best to win the trick, otherwise he may give a cheap trick to the opposition.

But what about *but?*

The exceptions occur when there are one or two high cards on your right:

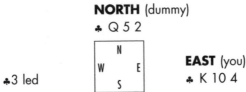

NORTH (dummy)

♣ Q 5 2

♣3 led

EAST (you)

♣ K 10 4

In positions of this type your aim in life is to insure that your king captures dummy's queen at some point. If dummy plays low, you must play the ten. And the same play would be correct if dummy held the jack instead of the queen.

Try some different arrangements of the missing cards, and you will see that these third-hand plays, aimed at controlling a high card on your right, often gain a trick and hardly ever lose.

QUIZ

1. Say whether each of the following doubles are takeout or penalty:

a) West	North	East	South
1♡	pass	2♡	pass
pass	dbl		

2. Suppose that with both sides vulnerable there is a one-heart opening bid on your left and your partner passes. Your hand is:

   ♠ A Q 10 5   ♡ 6   ◇ K J 5 3   ♣ A J 10 5

   What do you do if the action on your right is: (a) Pass? (b) One spade? (c) One notrump? (d) Two clubs? (e) Two hearts?

3. If your partner opens one heart, both sides vulnerable, and the next player bids one notrump, what should you bid with each of the following hands?

a) ♠ A 4 2	b) ♠ 7 6	c) ♠ Q 8 7 5 4 2
♡ 7 6	♡ A 4 2	♡ 8
◇ K J 7 2	◇ Q 8 7 4 2	◇ K 7 5 2
♣ J 10 8 3	♣ 7 3 2	♣ 8 6

4. Defending three notrump, your partner leads the spade three. You can see:

   Dummy
   ♠ J 5 2

   West leads the spade three and dummy plays low. What would you play as East with each of the following holdings?

a) ♠ K Q 4	b) ♠ K 10 4	c) ♠ A Q 10

   ┌─────────────────┐
   │ QUIZ │ ANSWERS │
   └─────────────────┘

1. (a) Takeout. Presumably a hand that was not strong enough to double the first time. This is a balancing action, usually desirable when the opponents find a fit and stop at a low level.

   (b) Penalty, since the bid was notrump. Partner is expected to pass unless he has a very weak hand and a long suit.

2. Double, takeout, in all cases. This shows opening values and length in the unbid suits. Case (c), after a one notrump response, is an exception to the normal rules. In all other circumstances a double of one notrump is for penalties. But the point is academic: you show a good hand and would be happy if partner chose to pass in the hope of a penalty.

3. (a) Double. Doubling one or two notrump is almost always desirable if you know your side has most of the high-card strength. The opponent has shown a hand equivalent to a one notrump opening, and his partner will have a very weak hand.
   (b) Two hearts, the same bid that you would have made without the intervening bid.
   (c) Two spades: obviously a weak hand with a long suit, and partner will usually pass. With a good hand you would have taken the opportunity to double.

4. (a) The queen, the lower of equals. If you play the king, partner will assume that you do not have the queen.
   (b) The ten, keeping the king to control the jack. If partner has the ace, the play will not matter. But if South has the ace, with or without the queen, it is vital to play the ten.
   (c) The ten. It will not matter what you do if your partner has the king. The play of the ten is safe. If you play the ace you will not be sure whether to continue the suit.

ESSENTIALS TO REMEMBER

1. Doubles are for penalties unless they are of low-level suit bids opposite a non-bidding partner.

2. Tend to make takeout doubles when short in the enemy suit, and penalty doubles when short in partner's suit.

3. With equal cards in defense, lead high but follow low.

4. In defense, play third hand high unless you are saving an honor to capture an honor on your right.

Almost all the bidding we have discussed so far has been rather peaceful: either the opponents have not bid at all, or they have done so at a low level.

Now we approach the high drama, moving, if you will, from peace to war. It is just like a commercial auction, in which one lot attracts little interest but the next can cause two enthusiasts to battle away determinedly with large sums on the line.

Here is a wild example:

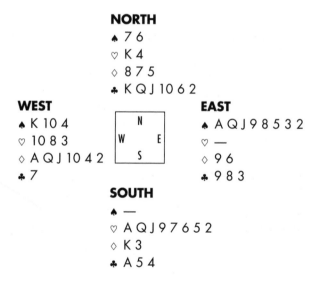

NORTH
♠ 7 6
♡ K 4
◇ 8 7 5
♣ K Q J 10 6 2

WEST
♠ K 10 4
♡ 10 8 3
◇ A Q J 10 4 2
♣ 7

EAST
♠ A Q J 9 8 5 3 2
♡ —
◇ 9 6
♣ 9 8 3

SOUTH
♠ —
♡ A Q J 9 7 6 5 2
◇ K 3
♣ A 5 4

South deals with both sides vulnerable and the bidding goes:

West	North	East	South
			1♡
2◇	3♣	4♠	5♡
5♠	6♡	6♠	??

Everyone becomes wildly excited as the auction develops. South is delighted because he has a partial fit with his partner's clubs and some control in all four suits. West is excited because he has a fit in the suit in which his partner jumped and a useful singleton in clubs. He has good reason to think that his partner is short in hearts. North is not exactly excited, but he is pleased to have the heart king, filling a gap in his partner's suit. And East feels aggressive when his partner shows a spade fit.

Look at the diagram and work out what will happen in the play. If South plays in a heart contract he will make all the tricks unless West leads the ace of diamonds. Six hearts is unbeatable and seven hearts might make: given the opportunity, South will draw trumps and throw his diamonds on North's clubs.

If East plays in spades he will be able to finesse in diamonds, trapping South's king. He will make all the tricks unless a club is led. Six spades is unbeatable and seven spades might make: given the opportunity East will draw trumps and use his partner's diamonds to discard club losers.

South and East both know that their 3 assets have tripled: they have been raised, admittedly after showing great length, so there must be at least a ten-card fit.

What happens next depends on the extent to which the players feel aggressive. There are three possibilities:

1. South is cautious, and passes six spades or doubles. Result: East-West make a small slam worth 1430 or 1660.

2. South is aggressive, bidding seven hearts, and East is cautious, passing or doubling. Result, depending on the opening lead: either East-West have a small profit, at most 200, or North-South score a grand slam, worth 2210, or more if doubled.

3. South is aggressive, bidding seven hearts, and East is aggressive, bidding seven spades. Result, depending on the opening lead: Either North-South have a small profit, at most 200, or East-West score a grand slam, worth 2210, or more if doubled.

It is easy to see from this that it is important to be aggressive. In such cases it pays heavily to play the hand. You may have a large profit, and you cannot have a large loss. If the laws allowed South to bid eight hearts (which they do not!) it would pay him to do so as insurance. He would lose a small penalty and would not risk having a grand slam made against him.

The guideline in wild competitive auctions, when both sides have a long suit and a fit, is: *when in doubt bid one more.*

The deal we have discussed is, of course, an extreme case. But the principle is valid at the four-, five-, and six-levels as well. You should be willing to accept a small penalty. And if someone is going to have a big score you would like it to be 'you' and not 'them.'

In this example both sides had chances of making a high-level contract. But in certain circumstances it may be right to bid when you have no chance whatever of making your contract.

Favorable vulnerability is the key. If the opponents are vulnerable and you are not, you can make a 'profit' by bidding aggressively and going down a few tricks – you are said to be **taking a save**. You concede a penalty, thus losing points but not as many as you would have done by being passive.

Assuming that the opponents are due to make their vulnerable contract (and you must be confident about that) the following table applies:

Opponents' Vulnerable Contract	You Profit by Going Down
Game	3 tricks (doubled)
Small slam	6 tricks (doubled)
Grand slam	8 tricks (doubled)

So if you are not vulnerable and the opponents are, bid aggressively. If you can find a good fit, nine cards or better in the combined hands, take a save. You will annoy the opponents, who will not wish to give up playing the hand for the sake of a relatively small penalty. Sometimes they will bid one more, and you will have a better chance to defeat them.

This is particularly attractive if you have the spade suit and the opponents bid four hearts. Put them to the test by bidding four spades. They are not likely to defeat you four tricks doubled, and if you can push them to five hearts you may even end up with a plus result.

Of course there is a down side to this: occasionally you will save and be doubled with a bad result. Either the penalty is bigger than you expected, or worse still, you would have defeated their contract (that is called a **phantom save**).

Suppose your hand as South is this:

♠ A K 10 9 8 7   ♡ 8 3   ◇ 10 6 5 2   ♣ 8

The vulnerability is favorable for you: they are vulnerable and you are not. Your left-hand opponent deals and the bidding goes:

West	North	East	South
1♡	pass	3♡	??

You should bid three spades. This is the perfect time to consider a save. With both opponents showing strong hands, your partner will not expect much from you except a long, strong suit. He will support you with a few spades, regardless of strength. You are pretty sure that he is very weak.

The bidding continues:

West	North	East	South
1♡	pass	3♡	3♠
4♣	4♠	pass	pass
6♡	pass	pass	6♠
dbl	all pass		

West thinks that he can make six hearts and you have no reason to disbelieve him. The penalty in six spades is likely to be much less than the value of their slam.

West leads the heart king and the dummy appears. As you expect, it has virtually no high-card strength.

NORTH
♠ 5 4 2
♡ 6
♢ J 9 8 7 3
♣ J 7 5 4

West leads the ♡K

SOUTH
♠ A K 10 9 8 7
♡ 8 3
♢ 10 6 5 2
♣ 8

West wins the first trick and shifts to the club king. East plays the club ten, encouraging a continuation. West plays the ace and you ruff.

There is no hurry to ruff your remaining heart, and that play would in fact be an error. You play the spade ace, West plays the jack and East the three.

Who has the queen?

There is a big clue if you think back to the bidding. West thought he could make six hearts so he did not expect to lose two immediate tricks in spades.

You conclude that the spade jack was a singleton. (That is right for other reasons too; see page 228.) So ruff your heart loser, lead dummy's last trump and finesse the ten when East plays low. As expected, West discards a heart. You play the spade king, removing the queen, and lead a diamond. East wins and leads a heart. You ruff and lead another diamond. Luckily the ace and king of diamonds crash together, and you make the rest of the tricks.

The result: down three, for a penalty of 500. If you had been less lucky you would have lost a trick or two more, but still much less than the value of their vulnerable slam: 1430 at most forms of scoring.

The complete deal was:

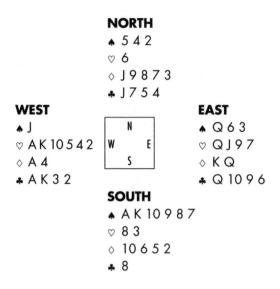

NORTH
- ♠ 5 4 2
- ♡ 6
- ◇ J 9 8 7 3
- ♣ J 7 5 4

WEST
- ♠ J
- ♡ A K 10 5 4 2
- ◇ A 4
- ♣ A K 3 2

EAST
- ♠ Q 6 3
- ♡ Q J 9 7
- ◇ K Q
- ♣ Q 10 9 6

SOUTH
- ♠ A K 10 9 8 7
- ♡ 8 3
- ◇ 10 6 5 2
- ♣ 8

Was the save worth it? Consider whether your opponents would have made six hearts.

West will certainly lose a spade trick, and has a little problem in the club suit. He can be expected to solve it, since South's bid shows that he has length in spades and the play marks him with two of the three missing hearts. In fact, once South has shown up with two hearts and at least two diamonds as well his spade length, he does not have room in his hand for four clubs anymore.

West should conclude that if anyone has a singleton club it must be South. So after drawing trumps he will play the ace and king of clubs. South discards, and West takes a 'marked' finesse against the jack to make the slam.

Remember that the save is usually indicated when the vulnerability is favorable. But it can be right when the vulnerability is equal — with neither side vulnerable or both sides vulnerable. Two down doubled is acceptable if the opponents were about to make a game, and four down doubled to save a slam. But a save at unfavorable vulnerability, when you are vulnerable and the opponents are not, is almost always unwise.

Now, as some famous Englishmen used to say, 'for something completely different.' Something we have not yet covered is — **covering**, i.e. playing an honor from your hand on an enemy honor that is led from your right. The idea of doing so is to promote a card in partner's hand:

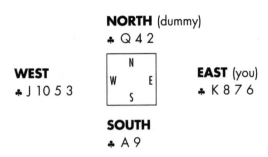

NORTH (dummy)
♣ Q 4 2

WEST
♣ J 10 5 3

EAST (you)
♣ K 8 7 6

SOUTH
♣ A 9

If declarer leads the queen of clubs from dummy, it is necessary for you to cover with the king. South will win his ace, but your partner's jack will now score a trick.

A rule of thumb, dating from the days of bridge's ancestor, whist, recommends that you 'always cover an honor with an honor.' It would be more sensible to say that you should 'often cover an honor with an honor,' although that does not help much. Some guidelines are needed.

Consider these examples of a lead from the dummy. You are East, defending four spades:

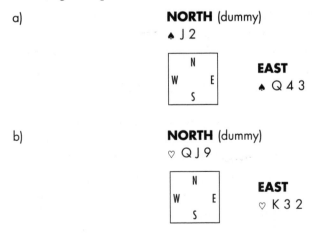

a)

NORTH (dummy)
♠ J 2

EAST
♠ Q 4 3

b)

NORTH (dummy)
♡ Q J 9

EAST
♡ K 3 2

c)

NORTH (dummy)
◊ 10 2

EAST
◊ K 4 3

With (a) you should not cover the jack if it is led from dummy. It is most unlikely to be right, and will often be wrong. As the opponents have chosen to play four spades they presumably have at least eight trumps. That leaves your partner with at most two, so covering will not help. You should never (remembering that in bridge 'never' means 'virtually never') cover with the queen of trumps. But if this was not the trump suit, and your partner could therefore have some length, you should cover the jack with the queen. The declarer might well have, for example, ace-king-ten-five, and covering will bring your partner's nine into play.

In (b) it would again be a mistake to cover the queen or the jack from dummy. If a sequence is led, delay covering: in this case, save the king to cover the jack. If you cover at once you may allow the declarer to take the ace and finesse for your partner's ten.

In (c) you should cover the ten if it is led, since you may well do your partner some good. If you consider that the declarer may have, for example, ace-queen-jack-five or ace-jack-five, you will see the point.

Now try these, with the suit led by South and the dummy on your left. Again, the contract is four spades.

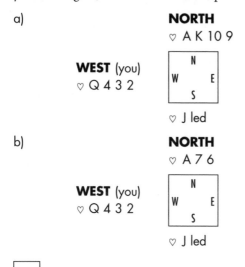

a)

NORTH
♡ A K 10 9

WEST (you)
♡ Q 4 3 2

♡ J led

b)

NORTH
♡ A 7 6

WEST (you)
♡ Q 4 3 2

♡ J led

c)

NORTH
♡ A K 10 8

WEST
♡ Q 3 2

♡ J led

In (a) it obviously cannot help your partner to cover, so play low. In (b) you should also play low. Since South would not lead an unsupported honor he probably has the ten. So this is the sequence situation: do not cover immediately if you can cover later. South might have jack-ten-six, for example.

You should cover in (c), hoping that your partner has the nine. If you fail to cover you will give declarer four tricks.

The situations in which an honor is led from the closed hand are rather difficult. You should tend to cover when dummy has a card in sequence with the card led, as in (c), but not when there are no such cards, as in (b).

QUIZ

1. The opponents are vulnerable and you are not. You are South and the bidding goes:

West	North	East	South
4♡	pass	6♡	??

What action would you take with each of the following hands?

a) ♠ K J 9 8 7 6 ♡ 5 ◇ 7 6 2 ♣ Q 9 2
b) ♠ K J 9 8 7 6 ♡ 5 ◇ K J 4 ♣ Q 9 2

2. Neither side is vulnerable. You are West and the bidding goes:

West	North	East	South
1♡	1♠	4♡	4♠
??			

What do you bid with each of the following hands?

a) ♠ 5   ♡ K J 9 8 6 4   ◇ 5 2   ♣ A K 9 3
b) ♠ 5 2   ♡ K Q 9 8 6   ◇ 5 2   ♣ A K 9 3

3. In each of the following diagrams, South is declarer in 3NT, and leads the ♡Q from his hand. Do you cover?

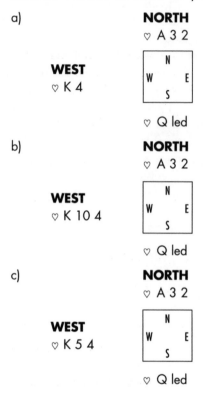

a)   **NORTH**
                             ♡ A 3 2

        WEST
        ♡ K 4

                             ♡ Q led

b)   **NORTH**
                             ♡ A 3 2

        WEST
        ♡ K 10 4

                             ♡ Q led

c)   **NORTH**
                             ♡ A 3 2

        WEST
        ♡ K 5 4

                             ♡ Q led

QUIZ ANSWERS

1. (a) You are guessing, but six spades is a good guess. It seems likely that six hearts will make, and if your partner has a few spades you will do fairly well.

(b) Another guess, but this time pass. You have a few cards that may take tricks so there is a danger that six spades will be a phantom save: down four tricks or more when six hearts would have failed.

2. (a) Five hearts. With a good fit, bid one more. There is a good chance you can make five hearts, and a considerable danger that the opponents can make four spades. You have a heart more than your partner expects.

    (b) Pass. You have a minimum opening bid, with the number of hearts your partner expects. Let him make the decision. If it is right to bid five hearts, he should be able to judge.

3. (a) Cover with the king, to make sure that your king does some useful work. If you play low, the king may have to be played on a low card.

    (b) Cover with the king, although it may not make any difference. Having the ten makes it safe to cover.

    (c) Do not cover. South probably has the jack, and perhaps the nine too. Wait to cover the jack.

ESSENTIALS TO REMEMBER

1. If both sides have a good fit, keep bidding. When in doubt, bid one more for luck especially if it is possible that your contract and their contract could both succeed.

2. If they are vulnerable and you are not, look for a save. Bid aggressively, especially if you have spades and they have hearts. Sometimes save at equal vulnerability, but virtually never at unfavorable vulnerability.

3. Cover an honor with an honor if it could help you or your partner, but never cover with the queen of trumps. If there is an equal honor visible on your right (say, jack led from queen-jack or jack-ten) wait and cover later. If the declarer leads an honor, tend to cover if dummy has a card in sequence with the card led.

Earlier this week we dealt with overcalls and takeout doubles, and how to respond to them. We did not discuss, however, the impact on the third player, whose partner opened the bidding. The impact is slight when there is a suit overcall:

West	North	East	South
1♡	1♠	??	

East's bids are almost the same as they would have been without the one-spade bid (but see next paragraph). He can bid two, three, or four hearts according to the strength of his hand. He can make a normal forcing response of two clubs or two diamonds, and his partner will expect at least 10 high-card points. A bid of one notrump is slightly stronger than it would have been: 8-10 points, with some strength in the enemy spade suit.

A new possibility is 'double'. Traditionally this was for penalties, suggesting that the opponents are in trouble. Typically, as we saw on page 111, it indicated a hand with length and strength in the opponent's suit, and shortness in opener's suit. But this situation is rare when the overcall is one of a suit, and not very common even at the two-level, so the meaning has disappeared in tournament play. It survives in some social games.

In the modern game, a double is 'negative', which means takeout. It indicates four cards or more in any unbid major suit. It will be exactly four if that suit can be bid at the one-level (as when the overcall is one heart, so that a one spade bid is still readily available). The strength of the double is 6 or more points, and 8 or more at the two-level. How high the negative double applies needs agreement. If the opener's partner has the hand to make a penalty double, he passes and hopes his partner will reopen with a double that he will then pass.

The big change occurs when there is a takeout double. Suppose that both sides are vulnerable and your partner opens one diamond, the next player doubles, and you are lucky enough to hold:

♠ A Q 4 3   ♡ Q 10 8 4   ◇ 7 2   ♣ A J 9

You have 13 high-card points, and your partner has 13, perhaps including an asset or two. You can certainly expect to make three notrump. But before you make that bid think a little more.

Your partnership seems to have 26 high-card points, give or take a point or two. The doubler seems to have about 13. There are 40 high-card points in the deck. So what does that leave for the doubler's partner?

Obviously, just about nothing. If he is lucky the fourth player will be looking at a queen or a jack.

So think about what will happen if the opponents play the hand (a good thing to think about in all competitive auctions). There is no reason to think that they have a normal fit, and they will do very badly in notrump, outgunned in points about 14 to 26.

You should therefore expect to do much better by defending against a doubled contract than by bidding game yourself. And you signal this in one word: **redouble**.

If a contract is played redoubled, the points at stake are roughly quadrupled. But that hardly ever happens. It is highly likely in this situation that the opponents will try another suit. Then, provided your partner doesn't frustrate your plan by bidding, you will double them. The penalty is almost sure to be bigger than the game you could have had.

The redouble is appropriate with almost all good hands following the opponent's double. The redouble shows at least 10 high-card points and hints at the possibility of a penalty.

Suppose instead the bidding goes:

West	North	East	South
			(you)
1◇	dbl	1♡	

What can you infer from this? Remember that with a good hand East would have redoubled. West can therefore assume that his partner has a moderate hand, with fewer than 10 high-card points and at least a five-card heart suit[1].

Similarly, East must be weak if he raises his partner. Any diamond bid, two, three, four, or five, denies a good hand in high cards. The more he bids, the more his assets have increased in value.

The opponents' bidding will often provide valuable clues in the play. Suppose you have this hand:

♠ J 8 3   ♡ Q 5   ◊ A Q J 10   ♣ 7 6 5 3

West	North	East	South
	(you)		(partner)
			1 ♠
dbl	??		

Virtually anything except a redouble, as we have seen, denies 10 high-card points. You have 10, so you redouble. Then next player bids two hearts and your partner passes — which is almost automatic since you may be aiming to double. West also passes, which is predictable since he knows he is outgunned in high cards. The bidding has been:

West	North	East	South
	(you)		(partner)
			1 ♠
dbl	redbl	2♡	pass
pass	??		

Your partner's opening promised a five-card suit, and it is time you showed a normal fit. You bid two spades, and your partner will know that you have a minimum redouble with some spade support. He bids four spades, which is optimistic, and then asks you to play the hand for him while he goes to the telephone.

---

1. Many modern players treat this bid as forcing, in which case East could be quite strong.

The heart king is led, and going round into your partner's seat you see:

NORTH
♠ J 8 3
♡ Q 5
◇ A Q J 10
♣ 7 6 5 3

West leads the heart king

SOUTH
♠ A K Q 10 4
♡ J 3
◇ 7 4 3
♣ A 9 4

You have to make ten tricks, and your first move, in a suit contract, is to count your losers. The result is not encouraging: two hearts, two clubs, and perhaps one in diamonds.

But if you remember the bidding there is some good news: West showed an opening bid with his takeout double, and it is highly likely that he has the king of diamonds. Even without the bidding you would assume that West had that vital card: if East has it your cause is lost.

If you count winners the answer is more encouraging: five spades, one club, and with the help of some finessing, four diamonds. That adds up to ten.

For the time being you are at the mercy of the opponents. West takes two heart tricks with the king and ace, and shifts to the club king. You win with the ace, and it is time for some detailed planning.

Is this a hand to draw trumps? In principle, yes. There is no ruffing you need to do in the dummy. But there is a catch. Can you see it?

Suppose that you draw trumps, in three or four rounds, and then turn to diamonds. You finesse the ten, and as you expect it will succeed. But what will you do then?

You want to finesse a second time in diamonds, and perhaps a third time. But the lead is now in the dummy and you have no way back. Your contract is doomed.

You forgot about your *entries*, and many intermediate players would make the same error. Since your plan is to take repeated diamond finesses you must make sure that you can reach your hand when you need to. The trump suit is the way back, so drawing trumps must give way. Diamonds have precedence.

At the fourth trick you must lead a diamond to the ten. It wins. Then play two rounds of trumps, ending in your hand, and take another diamond finesse. Now it is time to draw the remaining trump, again ending in your hand, and take the third and final diamond finesse to make your game.

The complete deal was:

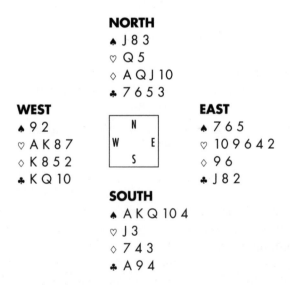

NORTH
♠ J 8 3
♡ Q 5
◇ A Q J 10
♣ 7 6 5 3

WEST
♠ 9 2
♡ A K 8 7
◇ K 8 5 2
♣ K Q 10

EAST
♠ 7 6 5
♡ 10 9 6 4 2
◇ 9 6
♣ J 8 2

SOUTH
♠ A K Q 10 4
♡ J 3
◇ 7 4 3
♣ A 9 4

One important point should be noted. East bid two hearts after the redouble, exactly as he would have done if North had passed. It will help West to know East's long suit, and the bid does not show any strength. The other three players all know that East has virtually no high-card strength.

It is important at the beginning of the play to think about entries. Where do you need them? Are there are enough? When will you use them? On the deal we have just played we needed entries to the South hand for diamond finesses. If we had not thought about that early enough all the entries would have vanished prematurely.

This deal shows one of the many reasons, apart from the usual one when ruffs are needed in the dummy, why it may be right to postpone the play of the trump suit.

For some practice in planning entries, consider this suit combination when West leads a club:

DUMMY
♣ A Q

YOU
♣ K 2

It is unfortunate that two of your honors will crash together. Since you have only doubletons you cannot take more than two tricks. But there are three ways to play, depending on circumstances:

1. If you need the lead in your hand immediately, you must play the queen and overtake with the king.

2. If you will need the lead in your hand later you must win with the ace in the dummy and play the two from your hand.

3. If you need the lead in dummy, both now and later, you can either win with the queen or win with the ace and drop the king.

Or suppose that in a notrump contract you have this combination:

DUMMY
♣ Q 7 2

YOU
♣ K J 4

The five of clubs is led. If you need to reach the dummy immediately you must play the queen, hoping, as is likely, that West has the ace. But if you will need the lead in dummy later you must play low from dummy and win with the king. If West has the ace he cannot prevent you scoring a trick later with the queen.

QUIZ

1. Your partner opens one heart and the next player doubles, for takeout. What will you bid with each of the following hands?

   a) ♠ A J 5 2   b) ♠ 4   c) ♠ 5 2
      ♡ —   ♡ A 8 7 3 2   ♡ 8
      ◊ K Q 9 5 2   ◊ 9 8 6 5 2   ◊ K Q J 10 5 4
      ♣ 10 7 6 2   ♣ 6 3   ♣ 9 8 4 2

2. Suppose the bidding goes:

West	North	East	South
			1♠
dbl	redbl	2♣	2◊
2♡			

   How many points does each player have?

3. Suppose clubs are led and you see:

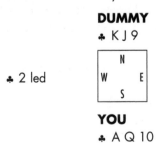

DUMMY
♣ K J 9

♣ 2 led

N
W   E
S

YOU
♣ A Q 10

   (a) How should you play if your main purpose is to save entries to the dummy?
   (b) How should you play if your main purpose is to save entries to your hand?

4. Suppose clubs are led and you see:

DUMMY
♣ Q J 5

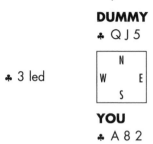

♣ 3 led

YOU
♣ A 8 2

How should you play if you want a later entry to the dummy?

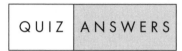

QUIZ | ANSWERS

1. (a) Redouble, showing at least 10 points, unrelated to hearts. You hope to double the opponents in something.
   (b) Four hearts. No redouble, so fewer than 10 high-card points. With a known ten-card fit the three assets have tripled.
   (c) Two diamonds. No redouble, so fewer than 10 high-card points. A misfit for hearts, and a good six-card suit.

2. West must have a very good hand to double and then bid again: perhaps 17-18 high-card points and a good heart suit. South must have a very weak opening bid, for he would normally pass two clubs to give his partner an opportunity to double. He is likely to have about 11 high-card points and at least five-five in spades and diamonds. North promised 10 high-card points with his redouble, and might have a point or two more. East has at least five clubs and his point count may be zero. Considering what the other players have shown, he probably has close to that.

3. (a) Play the nine from dummy and win with the ace. That leaves two possible entries to the dummy (and one to the closed hand).
   (b) Win cheaply in your own hand: ten over nine, queen over jack, or ace over king. This leaves two entries to your hand and, in case of need, one to the dummy.

In both cases you try to leave the remaining sequence of cards alternating between the two hands. It would be inflexible, and wrong, for example, to play the king from the North hand and the ten from the South hand.

4. Play low from dummy and win with the ace. The queen or jack will provide a later entry to the dummy.

ESSENTIALS TO REMEMBER

1. If your partner's opening suit-bid is doubled, redouble with 10 high-card points or more.

2. If there is a redouble on your right, show any unbid five-card suit. Show a four-card suit if you can do so at the one-level. Your hand is known to be very weak.

3. If your partner redoubles, you should nearly always pass, giving him a chance to double the enemy, unless you can yourself double.

4. Be careful to save entries in the hand in which you may need them later in the play.

We have already mentioned the **cuebid**, a bidding maneuver that comes in two quite different varieties — so different, indeed, that it would be better if they had different names.

If you raise your partner's one-spade opening bid to three spades and he bids four clubs, that is a high cuebid. It shows control of clubs, usually the ace, and suggests a contract of six spades. If partner just wanted to play game he would have bid four spades. Four clubs not only suggests a slam but also says something about the suit in which the cuebid is made.

Much more important is the low cuebid, which is a totally different animal. It is made in the enemy suit, says nothing about that suit, and carries this message: we have a game but I do not know which game.

One example of this was discussed under takeout doubles. If your partner doubles a suit, you can bid their suit to show a wish to head for game. Here is another example, with both sides vulnerable:

♠ 7 2   ♡ A Q 8 7 3   ♢ A K 9 8 2   ♣ 7

West	North	East	South
(you)		(partner)	
	1 ♣	1 ♠	pass
??			

Your partner should have close to an opening bid for his vulnerable overcall, so the combined hands should produce game. What game is a mystery. It might be spades, hearts, diamonds, or notrump. Only clubs is certainly eliminated.

You cannot bid two hearts, for that would not be forcing: it would suggest a weaker hand with better hearts. Normal actions are never forcing when the opponents open, so you need an abnormal action — a cuebid of two clubs to announce game prospects.

The cuebidder has usually added his values to those announced by his partner to reach a combined 26 or so. But what if partner has not bid?

West	North	East	South
(partner)		(you)	
	1♣	2♣	

The traditional meaning of this cuebid is what you might expect: a desire to reach game somewhere. This would mean a hand worth 26 points on its own. Such a hand is so rare that many players today use the bid for other purposes (see page 215).

The cuebid is equally useful for the partnership that opens the bidding:

♠ A Q 4 2   ♡ K J 5 4   ◊ 6   ♣ 10 8 7 6

West	North	East	South
	(you)		
			1NT
2◊	??		

Partner promised 16 points, so you have a combined 26. The cuebid of three diamonds is ideal, leaving the door open to four spades, four hearts, and three notrump.

Turning from theory to practice, you pick up the following hand. The opponents are vulnerable and you are not.

♠ Q 10 5 4   ♡ A Q J 6   ◊ K J   ♣ 10 7 6

West	North	East	South
	(you)		
			1♡
1♠	??		

This hand would be difficult to bid if West had passed (see page 216). As it is, you can make a rather different use of the cuebid by bidding two spades. This shows good support for hearts and the values to open the bidding[1]. A direct raise to four hearts would show a hand with fewer high cards but good assets. (Notice that other strong hands can be bid naturally, since a bid of two clubs or two diamonds would be strong and forcing.)

The complete bidding is:

West	North	East	South
	(you)		
			1♡
1♠	2♠	3♠	pass
pass	4♡	all pass	

As usual, you move into your partner's seat to play the hand. You see this:

NORTH
♠ Q 10 5 4
♡ A Q J 6
◇ K J
♣ 10 7 6

```
      N
  W       E
      S
```

West leads the ♠K

SOUTH
♠ —
♡ K 10 9 8 7 4
◇ 8 7 5 4
♣ A K 4

You notice that your partner was counting all his three assets when he opened the bidding. You ruff the opening lead. What do you do now? Take time out to think.

If you decided to lead a diamond, take a gold star. If you were going to lead a trump, go to the bottom of the class and listen carefully.

---

1. In tournament play, the hand may be slightly weaker, perhaps 10-12 points.

This is an example of the general principle we stated early in this book: *do not draw trumps if you need ruffs in the dummy.*

Look for a suit (not trumps, of course) in which you are longer than the dummy. In this case, the suit is diamonds.

In your hand you have a club loser and four possible diamond losers. It is not clear whether the king-jack will produce a trick, but you can certainly ruff two of your losers.

You lead a diamond and West plays low. You must guess what to do, in a position we shall discuss later. As it happens, it does not matter what you do on this deal because East has both the ace and the queen. You try the jack, and when he wins with the queen he shrewdly returns a trump. He can see that your plan is to ruff in the dummy and he wants to stop you. Usually one partnership wants to lead trumps and the other does not. Here it is the defenders who would like to draw them.

You win the trump lead, noting that West discards a spade, and lead another diamond. East wins and plays another trump, leaving you in control.

Win this trump lead in your hand and ruff a diamond in dummy. Enter your hand with a spade ruff and trump another diamond. Now another spade ruff allows you to draw the last trump and cash your ace-king of clubs. You will lose one club trick at the finish but you will have made your contract. The whole deal was:

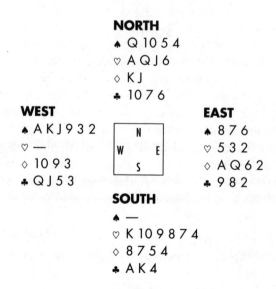

NORTH
- ♠ Q 10 5 4
- ♡ A Q J 6
- ◇ K J
- ♣ 10 7 6

WEST
- ♠ A K J 9 3 2
- ♡ —
- ◇ 10 9 3
- ♣ Q J 5 3

EAST
- ♠ 8 7 6
- ♡ 5 3 2
- ◇ A Q 6 2
- ♣ 9 8 2

SOUTH
- ♠ —
- ♡ K 10 9 8 7 4
- ◇ 8 7 5 4
- ♣ A K 4

If you had led even one round of trumps East would have been able to lead two more rounds of trumps. You would not have been able to ruff two diamonds in the dummy and you would have gone down.

Notice that it would have paid West to bid four spades. This would have been down one, and the bid might have pushed North-South to five hearts, down one. West allowed himself to be inhibited by the unfavorable vulnerability and forgot the guideline: when both sides have a fit, bid one more when in doubt.

Suppose the diamond layout had been slightly different:

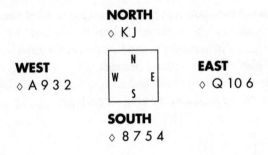

NORTH
◊ K J

WEST
◊ A 9 3 2

EAST
◊ Q 10 6

SOUTH
◊ 8 7 5 4

South leads a diamond and West plays low. South must guess. It will only matter if the ace and queen are in different hands, and the bidding and play may give him some idea about the position of the ace.

His guess would be very easy if West happened to be a beginner. When the diamond was led West would think for a few seconds. 'Should I win the trick with my ace?' he would ask himself.

If he then plays low he has given you the clue you needed. He must have been thinking about playing the ace, so you can play the king from dummy with confidence.

A more experienced player in the West position will play low promptly whether or not he has the ace. He knows that there is no hurry to take the ace, and he does not want to give you the hesitation-clue. He follows another general guideline: *in defense, play second hand low — and promptly.*

It helps to think ahead. Make up your mind ahead of time that you will play low.

Another example:

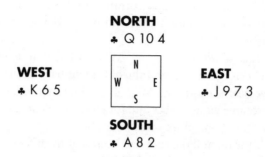

NORTH
♣ Q 10 4

WEST
♣ K 6 5

EAST
♣ J 9 7 3

SOUTH
♣ A 8 2

South leads the two, putting you to the test in the West seat.

If one trick in clubs is enough to beat the contract, by all means play the king. But in general you should observe the guideline for second hand: play low, and without hesitation.

That leaves South to guess, and he is quite likely to play the ten. East wins with the jack, and the king scores later.

QUIZ

1. Both sides are vulnerable. You hold as South:

    ♠ 3 2   ♡ A 8 7 4   ◇ A 9 3 2   ♣ K 7 6

West	North	East	South
1♠	2♣	2♠	??

What do you bid?

2. Both sides are vulnerable. You hold as North:

    ♠ 10 4 2   ♡ K Q 6   ◇ A J 7 2   ♣ K J 4

West	North	East	South
1♣	dbl	pass	2♣
pass	??		

What do you bid?

3. Defending four spades as West, you see this club layout:

NORTH
♣ K Q 10

WEST
♣ A 4 3

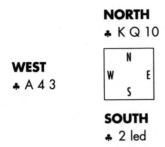

SOUTH
♣ 2 led

What will your normal plan of defense be?

4. Defending four spades as East, you see this trump layout:

NORTH
♠ A 7 6 2

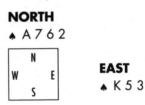

EAST
♠ K 5 3

If the spade two is led from the dummy, do you play the king?

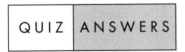

QUIZ ANSWERS

1. Three spades. The cuebid is appropriate, for there is an excellent chance of game. Partner's vulnerable overcall at the two-level suggests a good six-card suit and values for an opening bid. If he can bid three notrump, showing a spade stopper, we should have nine tricks — six in clubs and one in each of the other suits. Otherwise we can try for five clubs, and there is a slight chance that partner will bid hearts, finding a four-four fit.

2. Two notrump (or even three), showing a lack of interest in the major suits and a substantial holding in the enemy club suit. Partner's cuebid showed about an opening bid and a desire to reach game. We had almost enough to overcall one notrump instead of doubling. That would have shown a hand worth an

opening notrump bid, and guaranteed some strength in the enemy club suit.

3. You should normally plan to duck, twice if necessary, and with nonchalance. You hope that partner has the jack and that declarer will misguess the second time. If you take the ace, or perceptibly think about taking it, you help your opponent. (Take the ace, however, if taking it will guarantee the defeat of the contract.)

4. Play low promptly, following the second-hand guideline. If declarer had both the queen and jack, he would almost certainly have finessed. Your partner is sure to have one of the queen or jack, and taking your king will help your opponent.

ESSENTIALS TO REMEMBER

1. Use the low-level cuebid in the enemy suit to show a desire for game but doubt about the choice of game.

2. In defense, play second hand low automatically and quickly. Think ahead to look for the rare situations in which it is right to play second hand high.

It is time to review the theory discussed during the last six days, so answer the following review questions. If you score poorly on any question, you may need to reread the appropriate section.

REVIEW QUESTIONS

1. What is the worst vulnerability situation for an overcall?

2. Neither side is vulnerable, and your partner overcalls an opening one-spade bid with two diamonds. After a pass on your right, what do you bid with each of these hands:

a)	♠ 5 4 3	b)	♠ A J 5	c)	♠ 5 4 3 2
	♡ 6 2		♡ K J 4 2		♡ K J 2
	◇ J 7 3		◇ A 8		◇ A 8 5
	♣ A K 10 6 2		♣ 5 4 3 2		♣ A J 5

3. If the opponents bid one notrump-three notrump, what would you lead with each of the following hands?

a)	♠ 8 5 3	b)	♠ J 8 7 4 3	c)	♠ 10 9 5
	♡ 4 2		♡ Q J 10 9		♡ J 7 6 2
	◇ J 8 6		◇ 4 2		◇ Q 9 4 3
	♣ A Q 9 8 6		♣ 4 2		♣ K 6

4. If the opponents bid one spade-two spades-four spades, what would you lead with each of the following hands?

a)	♠ 6 5	b)	♠ J 5	c)	♠ 7 6 2
	♡ Q J 3		♡ Q 7 6 2		♡ K J 4
	◇ K Q 10		◇ 7 4 3		◇ Q 8 7 2
	♣ Q 8 7 4 2		♣ Q 7 6 2		♣ J 6 3

5. Suppose that your partner doubles an opening bid of one club. What do you expect him to have? And if your right-hand

opponent passes, what should you respond with each of the following hands?

a) ♠ K 8 7 4 2   b) ♠ 8 7 4   c) ♠ K 7 6 2
   ♡ Q 6 2   ♡ A 4   ♡ Q 9 5 3
   ◇ A 6 5   ◇ J 3 2   ◇ A K J
   ♣ 4 2   ♣ Q J 10 8 3 ♣ 7 2

6. What are the three kinds of defensive signal?

REVIEW ANSWERS

1. The most dangerous situation for an overcall occurs when you are vulnerable and the opponents are not.

2. With neither side vulnerable, your partner's two-level overcall suggests the values for an opening bid and at least a five-card suit (six is more likely). Your responses should be:
   (a) Three diamonds, a mild invitation to game. If partner can bid three notrump he will probably succeed.
   (b) Three notrump, the best chance for game. It is very unlikely that the opponents can take five club tricks, and everything else is controlled.
   (c) Two spades, the cuebid in the enemy suit to show a strong desire for game but uncertainty about the right game. Your partner may bid two notrump, showing a spade stopper and allowing you to bid three notrump.

3. (a) The club eight. Fourth from the top of a long, strong suit is the first choice against notrump. You hope that your partner will gain the lead and return a club, probably allowing you to score four tricks. On a very lucky day your partner will have the king.
   (b) The heart queen. Normally one leads a five-card suit rather than a four-card suit, but you should prefer a strong four-card suit, particularly one with an honor sequence, to a weak five-card suit.
   (c) The spade ten. Your four-card red suits are not promising, and leading one of them might well help the enemy. Leading the spade ten is unlikely to give anything away, and may do some good if your partner has length in spades.

4. (a) The diamond king. An honor sequence lead is good against a suit contract, and diamonds is better than hearts, partly because it sets up a trick quickly and partly because the ten is a useful supporting card.

   (b) A diamond. Try for a safe lead against a suit contract, and leading from scattered honors is unsafe. Which diamond you lead is a matter of partnership agreement.

   (c) A spade — any spade. This trump lead may do some good by cutting down a potential ruff in the dummy. Any other lead, from a lonely honor, may give away a trick.

5. You expect your partner to have opening values and either three-card or better support for each unbid suit or 17 or more high-card points (or both). He asks you to choose a suit.

   (a) Two spades, inviting game if the doubler has some extra strength. Remember that you could bid one spade on nothing at all, since you are forced to bid.

   (b) Pass. This is the exceptional situation in which you pass the double because you have length and strength in the enemy suit.

   (c) Two clubs. The cuebid shows strong game interest but doubt about the right game.

6. The normal signal denotes attitude: a high card shows a desire for a given suit to be played, a low card rejects a suit. Sometimes this cannot apply. If dummy has a long, strong suit, a defender helps his partner, for the purposes of a possible hold-up, by giving count — high with an even number of cards, low with an odd number. If neither of these apply, a suit preference signal is possible: a high card to ask for a high-ranking suit, a low card for a low-ranking suit.

It is now time to plug a gap in our bidding methods after an opening bid of one notrump. To do so we need the world's second-most-famous bridge convention: Stayman (the most famous is Blackwood).

Suppose that your partner opens the bidding with one notrump and you have one of the following hands:

a) ♠ K J 6 4   b) ♠ K J 6 4
    ♡ K J 6 4   ♡ K J 6 4
    ◊ 7   ◊ 7
    ♣ Q 8 7 2   ♣ 9 8 7 2

With (a) you know you have a combined 26 points, and therefore game. But what game? It might be spades, hearts, or notrump.

You need more information about partner's hand. You ask a question with a bid of two clubs.

This is the **Stayman** convention, or rather the Stayman question: 'Do you have a four-card major suit?'

There are three possible answers:

1. Two hearts, meaning 'I have four hearts' (perhaps five).

2. Two spades, meaning 'I have four spades' (perhaps five). (If you have both spades and hearts, bid whichever you like.)

3. Two diamonds, meaning 'I do not have four hearts or four spades.'

It is easy to see that this solves the problems of the two hands shown. You find out immediately whether there is a normal four-four fit in one of the major suits.

With (a) you raise a bid of two hearts or two spades to game. If the rebid is two diamonds, denying a major, you bid three notrump. In that case there is no normal fit in a major, and there is a strong presumption that the opener has some length in diamonds.

With (b) you invite game. If the rebid is two hearts or two spades you raise to three, giving partner the chance to stop with a minimum notrump bid. If the rebid is two diamonds you bid two notrump, again leaving the final decision to partner. This shows the same 9-point hand you would have shown with an immediate raise to two notrump.

If you think game is possible or certain you should use Stayman on virtually any hand that contains at least one four-card major suit.

Stayman provides a solution for other hands with invitational strength[1]. Suppose that your partner opens one notrump and you have:

♠ A Q 8 6 5   ♡ 4 2   ◊ 10 4 3   ♣ Q 6 5

You would like to bid spades, but how many? Two spades would show a weak hand, commanding partner to pass. You are too strong for that. Three spades would show that you could count the combined 26 points needed for game. You are slightly too weak for that.

To suggest game in spades, but not guarantee it, you bid two clubs, Stayman, and then bid spades at the cheapest level. Over two

---

1. So far, this book has described traditional responses to one notrump. These are still in use in many social games, but modern players virtually all use the **transfer bids** devised by Oswald Jacoby. In this method, a two diamonds response to one notrump shows at least five hearts, and two hearts shows at least five spades. The opener virtually always bids one step up, landing in his partner's long suit. This has the advantage that the strong hand nearly always becomes the declarer, and the opening lead comes around to the strength.

The transfer guarantees that the responder will have another chance to bid. He may follow with one of the following actions: two notrump, showing a balanced hand and inviting game in notrump or the promised major; three notrump, asking opener to choose between game in notrump or the promised major; three of the major (inviting) or four of the major (to play); or a new suit, forcing, looking for game and perhaps slam.

If you use transfers, a response of two spades does not mean spades, since a hand with spades would bid two hearts. It usually means, by agreement, length in the minor suits.

hearts or two diamonds you bid two spades, but over two spades you bid four spades.

There is, unfortunately, a gray area in responding to notrump. People have different ideas about some other minor-suit bids, and they must be discussed with each partner before you play:

1. Three clubs and three diamonds. The modern style is to use these as weak bids, with a six-card or longer suit and no interest in game. The opener is required to pass.

   The traditional style is for these to be strong and forcing, hinting at a slam. In that case two clubs, Stayman, followed by three clubs would be weak.

2. Two diamonds. Without any agreement, this is weak in the same way as two hearts and two spades. Partner must pass.

Now for some action. Both sides are vulnerable, and your partner deals and bids one notrump. Your hand is:

♠ A 7 5 4   ♡ Q 6   ◇ K 5 2   ♣ K 10 8 2

What do you bid?

It would not be wrong to bid three notrump, but it is slightly better to look for a normal spade fit. So you bid two clubs, Stayman.

Your partner bids two spades, as you hoped, and of course you bid four spades. Moving around the table to play the hand for your lazy partner you see:

NORTH
♠ A 7 5 4
♡ Q 6
◇ K 5 2
♣ K 10 8 2

West leads the ♡ J

```
      N
  W       E
      S
```

SOUTH
♠ Q J 6 2
♡ A 4
◇ A 7 4
♣ A Q 9 7

Count your losers, leaving the trump suit until last. You may lose a heart trick: you will play the queen now, and lose a trick if East has the king. Eventually you will lose a diamond trick. Clubs look safe, but there may be a small problem with the jack.

Is there any way to avoid a trump loser? No, unless the defense errs. Try it with any layout you like. If, for example, West has a doubleton king, leading the queen or jack will do no good unless West makes a mistake and does not cover with the king.

Since you must resign yourself to losing one trick in trumps, you should concentrate on not losing two. There is no problem if there is normal three-two division of the opponents' five cards: the ace will take a trick, the queen-jack will take one trick, and the opponents will take a trick.

You must worry about a four-one split. If West has four trumps including the king you can do nothing about it. But suppose that East has four trumps to the king. You can handle that if you make sure that the king does not capture the queen or the jack.

The wrong play, therefore, is to lead the queen or jack. That insures that the player with the king will be able to use it effectively. The right play is to start with the ace, then lead toward the queen-jack, twice if necessary.

Now we must play. The only hope to avoid a heart loser is that West has the king. So we play the queen, but East covers with the king and we win with the ace.

Now we carry out our plan in the trump suit by leading to the ace. This would pick off a singleton king if there happened to be one, but both opponents play low trumps. Now we play a trump from the dummy, and East plays low and we put on the queen. West discards a heart, and we are glad we played the trumps this way. If we had made the mistake of leading the queen of spades early, East would have scored two trump tricks.

We are now looking at this:

NORTH
♠ 7 5
♡ 6
◇ K 5 2
♣ K 10 8 2

SOUTH
♠ J 6
♡ 4
◇ A 7 4
♣ A Q 9 7

We need to play another spade from the dummy, but the lead is in the wrong hand. What entry should we use?

It would be wrong to play a club, for reasons that will become clear later. Instead play a diamond to the king. Then we lead another trump from dummy, and East wins with the king. He leads a diamond, and we win with the ace.

The spade jack removes East's last trump and we are in control. But there is one small problem. How should we play the clubs?

In a way, this is like the spade suit: it is easy with a three-two split of the defenders' cards. We must worry about the possibility that one defender has four clubs including the jack. The first move is to lead the ace (or the queen), which does not commit us.

Now we have to make a commitment. Which defender has the majority of the missing clubs? We cannot be sure, but the odds favor West. The clue is that we know the spade distribution: East had four and West one. It is quite unlikely that West began with two singletons.

The next play should therefore be the high honor from the South hand. It turns out to be right, for East discards a diamond. Now we have a **marked finesse** in clubs. We lead a club to the ten with total confidence, since East did not have any clubs on the previous trick.

The clubs take us to ten tricks, and we are content to surrender a trick in each red suit at the finish. The complete deal was this:

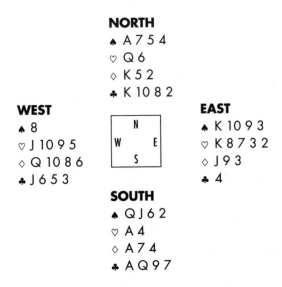

NORTH
♠ A 7 5 4
♡ Q 6
◊ K 5 2
♣ K 10 8 2

WEST
♠ 8
♡ J 10 9 5
◊ Q 10 8 6
♣ J 6 5 3

EAST
♠ K 10 9 3
♡ K 8 7 3 2
◊ J 9 3
♣ 4

SOUTH
♠ Q J 6 2
♡ A 4
◊ A 7 4
♣ A Q 9 7

It should now be clear why it was right to use diamonds rather than clubs to reach the dummy at the fourth trick. Not only would you have lost your flexibility in clubs, losing your option to trap West's jack, but you would have given East a chance for a club ruff. Other things being equal, you should use the entry that is least likely to give the enemy a ruff.

The hardest part of this deal was knowing how to manage the spade suit. Combinations in which you have at least one honor in each hand are harder than those we discussed early in this book: the simple low-to-high rule does not apply. In reading the next two pages, which are difficult and important, it may help you to get out a deck of cards, separate the club suit, and try out the combinations.

Life is fairly easy when you have four of the five honor cards (ace-king-queen-jack-ten):

a) ♣ A Q 3 2   b) ♣ A K 4 2   c) ♣ A K 6 4 2
    ♣ J 10 5 4   ♣ J 10 5 3   ♣ J 10 5 3

In each case your main concern is whether the lone honor held by the opposition will take a trick. In each case you could lead the jack (or ten) and take a finesse.

In each case that would be wrong, but only slightly. In general it is right to postpone finesses if it is convenient.

In (a) you want to trap the king, and you make the assumption that it is on your left. You should lead low to the queen. If this wins you return to your hand in another suit and lead an honor to finesse. The postponement helps if there is a singleton king on your left. The immediate finesse would be correct if you held the nine in either hand, or if you lacked a convenient entry back to your hand.

In (b) you want to trap the queen. Missing five including the queen you normally plan to finesse: with a normal three-two split the queen is likely to be in the three-card holding. Again, you should postpone the issue if you can by cashing the ace or king, returning to your hand in another suit to lead the jack or ten for the finesse. Here also, finesse at once lacking a reentry.

In (c) you should certainly start with the ace or king. But whether you should then play the other top card, hoping the queen will fall, or reenter your hand to take a finesse is a virtual guess unless there is a clue from the bidding and play.

There is a kernel of truth in the old rule of thumb, dating back to the beginning of the last century: eight ever, nine never. This means that when missing the queen you should finesse with eight cards in the combined hands (which is true in principle) but not finesse with nine cards. The last part is a guess, and no rule is needed. The only rule we need is: *missing five cards, tend to finesse for the queen.*

Now look at the same three combinations with the ten removed:

d) ♣ A Q 3 2   e) ♣ A K 4 2   f) ♣ A K 6 4 2
   ♣ J 6 5 4   ♣ J 6 5 3   ♣ J 7 5 3

With only three of the honors the situation is quite different. We are not concerned to trap an opposing honor but rather to score our own high cards. Leading the jack, either quickly or one trick later, would be a blunder: you would be hurt, not helped, if the next player covered your jack with his honor.

This is obvious enough in (e) and (f). You would like to score a trick with the jack, and you cannot do that by leading it. You should play the ace and king hoping the queen will fall. This is slightly better than a fifty-fifty chance in (f), but distinctly worse in (e).

The play in (d) is a little more complicated, and very important to understand. To avoid losing a trick in the suit you must take the first three tricks with high cards. You cannot manage this if the enemy king scores, or if the king captures one of your honors. You must assume that the king is on your left, so you start by leading low from your hand and finessing the queen. If this wins you play the ace, hoping the king will fall. If it does, your jack wins the third trick. If not, there was nothing you could do.

This example, and the trump suit in the deal we played, are examples of this general guideline: *when you have three honors, or fewer, concentrate on making tricks with your honors.*

In other words, do not worry about trapping their high cards. (However, this assumes that you do not have the nine. That can be a useful card and change the picture.)

Three more examples. In each case you want to make three tricks, and you have plenty of entries in other suits.

g) ♣ A K 3 2 h) ♣ A 5 4 3 i) ♣ K 5 4 3

♣ J 4 ♣ Q J 2 ♣ Q J 2

With (g) you are sure of two tricks with the ace and king. The only way to score the jack is to lead toward it from the dummy immediately, hoping the queen is on your right. If you had the ten you would be willing to finesse, playing for the queen to be on your left, not your right.

Example (h) is rather like the trump situation in the deal we played above. Leading the queen or jack would be a mistake, unless your aim in life is to take two tricks quickly. If you want to score three tricks you should lead low from the dummy to the queen or jack. If that wins, return to dummy in another suit and repeat the process, saving the ace. If it loses you can hope that the missing cards are evenly divided. Again, if you had the ten it would be quite different. You would play for the king to be on your left, not your right.

Example (i) is very difficult, and almost all average players misplay it. The secret of this and similar combinations, with seven cards missing the ace and ten, is to lead twice toward the hand with two honor cards. Here you lead low from the dummy to the queen (or jack). If that wins, go back to dummy in another suit and lead another low card. If you are lucky, the ace will pop up on your right because that player began with a doubleton ace. That is an extra chance for you. You are still safe if the opponents' six cards are split three-three.

QUIZ

1. Your partner opens one notrump. The opponents do not bid. Plan your bidding with each of the following hands:

    a) ♠ A Q 7 6 2   b) ♠ K 7 6 2   c) ♠ 7 6 3 2
       ♡ K J 6 2   ♡ A 8 6 3 2   ♡ 8 5 3 2
       ◇ 7   ◇ 7   ◇ 9 8 6 5
       ♣ 10 7 2   ♣ 10 7 2   ♣ 4

2. The bidding goes:

West	North	East	South
		pass	1NT
pass	2♣	pass	2♡
pass	2NT		

   What does North have?

3. Plan your play with each of the following combinations. You have entries to each hand, and need the number of tricks shown.

    a) ◇ A J 6 4 2   b) ◇ K J 4 2   c) ◇ A J 4 2
       ◇ Q 5 3   ◇ Q 5 3   ◇ Q 3

    Five tricks   Three tricks   Three tricks

1. (a) Bid two clubs, Stayman, planning to bid game[2]. If partner bids a major, raise to game. If he bids two diamonds, jump to three spades. This shows a five-card suit, and partner will either raise, with three-card support, or bid three notrump, with a doubleton spade.

   (b) Bid two clubs, Stayman. If partner bids two hearts, raise to four hearts. You have a nine-card fit and your 2 assets have doubled. If partner's response is two spades your assets are stable. Raise to three spades, inviting game. If the rebid is two diamonds, there is no fit and your assets vanish. Bid two hearts, non-forcing but invitational.

   (c) Bid two clubs, Stayman, and pass the rebid. There is a very good chance that this will get you to a better contract than one notrump would be. If the rebid is two spades or two hearts we have found a normal eight-card fit. If the rebid is two diamonds there is a good chance (better than fifty-fifty) of a normal fit.

2. This is an invitation, showing the same values as a direct raise to two notrump. It implies interest in a major suit, which must be spades. If the opener has spades as well as hearts (as he might) he can bid three spades (minimum) or four spades (maximum). Lacking spades he will pass (minimum) or bid three notrump (maximum).

3. (a) Hope that there is a doubleton king on your left. Lead low from your hand and finesse the jack. If it wins, play the ace and hope the king falls.

   (b) Lead from your hand to the jack (or king). If it wins, return to your hand in another suit and lead another small card. This gains against a doubleton ace on the left, and you are still safe with a three-three split.

---

2. Alternatively, using transfers, bid two hearts, showing spades and follow with three hearts.

(c) You must try to score tricks with the ace, queen and jack. This is virtually impossible if the king is on your left, and you should hope it is on your right. Hope for something like this:

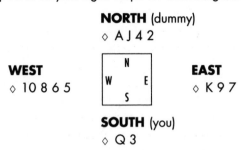

NORTH (dummy)
◊ A J 4 2

WEST
◊ 10 8 6 5

EAST
◊ K 9 7

SOUTH (you)
◊ Q 3

Lead low from dummy. If East takes the king you have your three tricks. If he plays low, following the second-hand-low guideline, you win the queen. Then you duck a round. Eventually you play the ace to drop the king, and the jack scores. If East has more than three cards including the king you can do nothing but hope he makes the mistake of playing second hand high, giving you what you want.

ESSENTIALS TO REMEMBER

1. In response to one notrump, two clubs is Stayman, asking for a major suit.

2. If your partner uses Stayman, bid a major if you can, and two diamonds if you cannot.

3. Stayman followed by a bid at the two-level is a game invitation.

4. Other minor-suit responses to one notrump (two diamonds, three clubs, and three diamonds) need discussion with your partner[3] (see page 153).

5. If you have four of the five honor cards in a suit (ace-king-queen-jack-ten) and are missing the king or queen try to trap the missing card. With three of the five, concentrate on scoring tricks with your three honors.

6. If you have a four-three fit missing the ace and ten, lead toward the hand with more honors, twice if necessary.

---

3. If you and your partner have agreed to use transfer bids, a response of two diamonds means hearts and a response of two hearts means spades. A subsequent new suit is forcing. Other bids invite.

When you have 13 points or more, including assets, the one-level opening bids we have discussed will be appropriate almost all the time. But in a tiny number of cases — perhaps one deal in twenty — you will be too strong. You will have good reason to fear that if you open one of a suit, and your partner passes, you will miss a game.

Your partner will respond to a one-bid in a suit with 6 points, allowing for the possibility of a 20-point opening. If you open one of a suit with more, and you sometimes do, you may miss a game if your partner has a few points, but not quite enough to respond.

When your hand is so strong that you are sure, or almost sure, of game, you must do something else. There are two opening bids that carry this message, and the most important of them is **two clubs**.

This is a totally artificial bid. (Like Stayman. The club suit is sometimes given an artificial meaning because it is rarely the right spot for a game.)

Two clubs announces game intentions, and game will almost always be reached. Suppose you deal yourself:

♠ K Q J 10 9   ♡ A Q J 8 7   ◊ 5   ♣ A K

This is 23 points, including assets, and 23 is usually enough to have good prospects of game even if partner is very weak. Here you hope to have a normal fit in spades or hearts. If that can be found you have a good chance to make ten tricks, losing one spade trick, one heart, and one diamond.

So you start the action with two clubs, signaling game intentions. Your partner is expected to bid two diamonds, which is also artificial and in principle negative. It suggests (but does not guarantee) a weak hand. If instead he makes a positive bid of two hearts (or two spades, or three clubs, or three diamonds), he shows a strong five-card or longer suit with moderate strength, and a minimum of about 8 points.

Your partner does bid two diamonds. Since you have already announced great strength you can now bid slowly, showing both your suits. You start with two spades, choosing the higher-ranking five-card suit just as you would have done at the one-level. (If you had chosen to open one with this hand, it would have been one spade.)

You have promised game, and your partner is not allowed to pass: your bid is completely forcing. If your partner is very weak he will now bid three clubs. (The cheaper available minor suit is usually used as a 'second negative'.)

He does bid three clubs and you bid three hearts, asking him to choose between your suits, and he puts you back to spades at the three level. You go to four spades, ending the bidding, which was:

South	North
(you)	(partner)
2♣	2♦
2♠	3♣
3♡	3♠
4♠	pass

Four spades turns out to be a struggle, because the dummy your partner produces is, predictably, very weak indeed. The whole deal is:

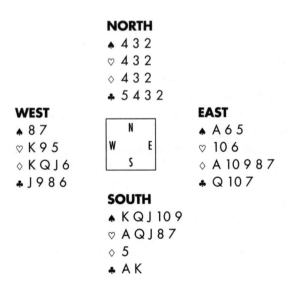

NORTH
♠ 4 3 2
♡ 4 3 2
♦ 4 3 2
♣ 5 4 3 2

WEST
♠ 8 7
♡ K 9 5
♦ K Q J 6
♣ J 9 8 6

EAST
♠ A 6 5
♡ 10 6
♦ A 10 9 8 7
♣ Q 10 7

SOUTH
♠ K Q J 10 9
♡ A Q J 8 7
♦ 5
♣ A K

Advanced players will note that to make four spades you must be very careful to keep control of the trump suit. The defenders will lead diamonds on the first trick and at every opportunity thereafter, rightly aiming to weaken your control of the trump suit.

You ruff the second diamond lead and drive out the ace of spades. They force you to trump another diamond and you draw one more trump to reach this delicate position:

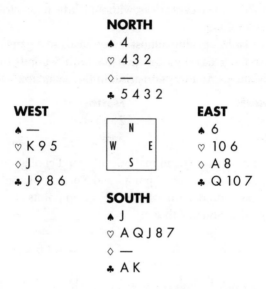

NORTH
♠ 4
♡ 4 3 2
◇ —
♣ 5 4 3 2

WEST
♠ —
♡ K 9 5
◇ J
♣ J 9 8 6

EAST
♠ 6
♡ 10 6
◇ A 8
♣ Q 10 7

SOUTH
♠ J
♡ A Q J 8 7
◇ —
♣ A K

You need to establish your hearts, but how? If you draw the missing trump the defenders will take two diamond tricks when they gain the lead with the heart king. If you play the ace of hearts now and follow with the queen or jack West will win and play a third round, allowing his partner to ruff.

The winning play, a very difficult one, is to lead the queen or jack of hearts in the position shown. If West takes his king, dummy's trump will take care of another diamond lead. And if West ducks you can safely play the ace and another heart.

In real life you need not worry about holding the North hand shown. Ely Culbertson, the dominant bridge personality of the thirties, once offered a prize for anyone who could prove that he had been dealt such a hand. Nobody collected.

Exactly how strong you must be to open two clubs is a tricky question. You should always make the bid with 25 points; usually with 23-24; very rarely with fewer. In borderline cases consider whether your hand is likely to make game if partner is very weak. If the South hand above were changed, and the long suits were diamonds and clubs instead of spades and hearts, a two clubs opening would be too aggressive. You could not expect to make game in a minor suit, requiring eleven tricks, without a little high-card strength in your partner's hand.

The two clubs opening almost always leads to a game. (Or to a slam. If responder has a moderate hand, with 8 points or more, a slam is very likely.) An exception arises in this sequence:

South	North
2♣	2◊
2NT	pass

South shows a notrump hand that was just good enough for the two clubs opening. He has 23 or 24 points, and North is allowed to pass if he is very weak indeed: perhaps one jack, or no points at all.
Suppose you deal yourself this:

♠ A Q 5   ♡ A Q   ◊ K J 3   ♣ A J 8 4 3

This is 22 points, including an asset for clubs. This is not quite enough for two clubs, which usually starts at 23. It is certainly too strong to open at the one-level. The solution is to open two notrump.

This shows a balanced hand with 21-22 points, and partner will act accordingly. His options, corresponding closely to the responses to one notrump, are:

1. Pass. This is very weak, 0-3 points, perhaps 4.

2. Three notrump shows 4-10 points and no interest in the major suits.

3. Three clubs is Stayman, just like two clubs in response to one notrump. The opener bids a major if he can, and three diamonds if he cannot.

4. Three spades[1], or three hearts (rarely three diamonds), shows at least a five-card suit, and doubt about the final contract. Opener raises with three cards or more, or bids three notrump with a doubleton.

5. Four spades or four hearts shows at least a six-card suit, fixing the final contract.

Now turn from theory to practice. You deal yourself:

♠ A K 8   ♡ K Q 9   ◊ A 10 9 3   ♣ A K 7

What do you bid?

Two clubs. The strong artificial opening is usually right with 23 points, and always right if, as here, the hand is balanced. As nearly always happens, partner makes the artificial response of two diamonds.

What now?

Two notrump, of course. This shows the balanced 23-24-point hand, and partner will bid unless he is desperately weak. His options are similar to those following a two-notrump opening.

He bids three clubs. What do you do?

Three diamonds, denying a major suit. Three clubs was Stayman.

Partner, who is the captain in this auction, as he normally is opposite a hand that is known to be balanced, picks three notrump. The complete bidding, with the opponents silent, was:

South	North
(you)	(partner)
2♣	2◊
2NT	3♣
3◊	3NT
pass	

---

1. Again, using modern transfer bids, respond three diamonds with heart length and three hearts with spade length.

West leads the heart seven and you see:

NORTH
♠ J 6 5 3
♡ 5 4
◇ K J 8 5 2
♣ 8 6

SOUTH
♠ A K 8
♡ K Q 9
◇ A 10 9 3
♣ A K 7

North used Stayman hoping for a four-four spade fit, but did not find it.

At first sight it seems that nine tricks will be easy. You expect to make, at least, four diamond tricks, one heart, and two tricks in each black suit. All the suits except clubs might produce another trick.

You play a low heart from dummy, East plays the jack, and you win with the king.

When everything seems easy, ask yourself this question: what can go wrong?

The heart suit is a threat. You cannot, obviously, afford to lose four heart tricks and a diamond trick.

You should know the heart position. If East held the ace he would have played it. And if he had begun with jack-ten he would have played the ten. We conclude, therefore, that West has the ace-ten, and he probably began with five or six hearts.

You can see what will happen if East gains the lead. He will lead a heart, and West will take at least four heart tricks to defeat you.

But that can only happen if East gains the lead. You are entirely safe if West gains the lead, since a heart lead will come around to your remaining high honor.

To avoid the danger that East will have the lead, you must make an **avoidance play**.

Play the diamonds in a way that will be safe. Lead to the king at the second trick, and finesse against East. If this loses to the queen you are safe. And if it wins you will make at least ten tricks. This is what happens, for the complete deal is:

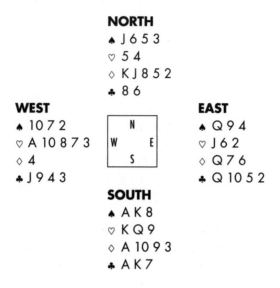

NORTH
♠ J 6 5 3
♡ 5 4
◇ K J 8 5 2
♣ 8 6

WEST
♠ 10 7 2
♡ A 10 8 7 3
◇ 4
♣ J 9 4 3

EAST
♠ Q 9 4
♡ J 6 2
◇ Q 7 6
♣ Q 10 5 2

SOUTH
♠ A K 8
♡ K Q 9
◇ A 10 9 3
♣ A K 7

If you play the diamonds in any other way, East will have a chance to win a trick and will beat you with a heart return.

Notice that West has the hearts, but East's is the dangerous hand. This not always true:

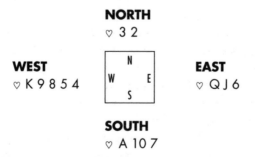

NORTH
♡ 3 2

WEST
♡ K 9 8 5 4

EAST
♡ Q J 6

SOUTH
♡ A 10 7

You are playing three notrump and the heart five is led. You allow the jack to win and then hold up again when the queen is led. You win the ace on the third round, noting that West played the four and then the eight.

You are sure that West has the two missing hearts. His is the dangerous hand. If he has no entry, it will be safe to allow East to gain the lead.

QUIZ

1. Plan your bidding as dealer with each of the following hands:

a)		b)		c)	
♠ K Q J 4		♠ A Q J		♠ A K 5	
♡ A		♡ K J 10 3		♡ —	
◊ A 2		◊ K 3 2		◊ A K Q 10 3	
♣ A K Q 7 6 5		♣ A K J		♣ K Q J 9 2	

2. If your partner opened two notrump, how would you respond with each of the following hands?

a)		b)		c)	
♠ A 9 8 7 4 3		♠ A Q J 5 2		♠ A J 4	
♡ 6		♡ K 7 4 3		♡ Q 8 7 2	
◊ 7 2		◊ 5		◊ A 10 3	
♣ 7 6 5 2		♣ 9 8 3		♣ J 6 5	

3. You are South in three notrump. If the dangerous hand is (i) West, (ii) East, how would you play each of the following combinations (you may lead first from either hand)?

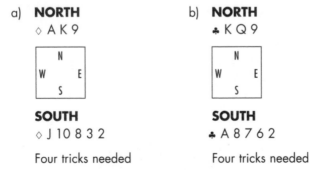

a) **NORTH**
   ◊ A K 9

   N
   W   E
   S

   SOUTH
   ◊ J 10 8 3 2

   Four tricks needed

b) **NORTH**
   ♣ K Q 9

   N
   W   E
   S

   SOUTH
   ♣ A 8 7 6 2

   Four tricks needed

4. West leads the six of diamonds against your three notrump contract. Plan your play in diamonds with the following layout if you expect to lose the lead to (i) West or (ii) East.

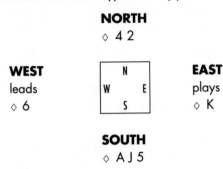

NORTH

◊ 4 2

WEST

leads

◊ 6

EAST

plays

◊ K

SOUTH

◊ A J 5

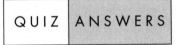

QUIZ ANSWERS

1. (a) Bid two clubs, artificial. Later, if possible, bid three clubs and then three spades. Bid your suits in a natural order.

   (b) Bid two notrump, showing 21-22 points and a balanced hand.

   (c) Two clubs, artificial. Later bid three diamonds and four clubs. Support spades if partner bids them.

2. (a) Four spades[2], selecting the final contract, with a guaranteed normal fit. You are the captain.

   (b) Three clubs, Stayman. You plan to bid a slam in spades, hearts or notrump. Asking partner for a major suit is the first step.

   (c) Six notrump. You can count 33 points, and notrump is entirely satisfactory.

3. (a) (i) Finesse the nine, playing the ace or king first if convenient.

   (ii) Play the ace and king and then a third diamond. If East wins this trick there was nothing you could do but you have guarded against a doubleton queen on your right.

---

2. Using transfers, bid three hearts and then four spades.

(b) (i) Lead low from your hand and if West follows play the nine, guarding against a four-card holding with West.

(ii) Make the normal play of the king and queen, hoping that East does not have four cards including both missing honors.

4. (i) Win with the ace, so that you are protected in the suit if West gains the lead.

(ii) Hold up the ace as long as possible, so that East will have no more diamonds to lead later.

ESSENTIALS TO REMEMBER

1. Open two clubs, strong and artificial, with any hand on which you expect to make game even if partner is very weak. Bid it with 23 points or more (except perhaps when your suit is a minor).

2. If partner opens two clubs respond two diamonds, artificial, unless you have a long, strong suit.

3. A two-notrump opening shows 21-22 points. With slightly better-balanced hands, 23-24, bid two clubs and then two notrump. Partner can raise, bid three clubs Stayman to ask for a major, or bid a suit to ask for three-card support[3].

4. In planning the play, think about which opponent may get the lead and whether one opponent is more dangerous than the other.

5. You can now bid any balanced hand as opener:

0-12   Pass.
13-14 Open one of a suit and then make minimum notrump bid.
15-17 Open one notrump.
18-20 Open one of a suit and then jump in notrump.
21-22 Open two notrump.
23-24 Open two clubs, then bid two notrump.
25-27 Open two clubs, then bid three notrump.

---

3. Or use a transfer if available.

When Alice encountered the Sheep in the Looking-Glass World she found that one egg was more expensive than two. Bridge theory is even more topsy-turvy: a two diamonds opening is weaker than one diamond, and the same is true of any higher opening suit bid.

Normal hands open at the one-level. Strong hands open two clubs or two notrump. Weak hands, if they have a long, strong suit, make opening bids such as two diamonds, three hearts, four spades, or five clubs.

These are called **preemptive bids**, an attempt to buy into the auction before the enemy gets going. The French have a more descriptive word: *barrage*.

Such bids have a double purpose. They make the bidding easy for partner, since he knows he is facing a long, strong suit with little or no outside strength. But more important, they set the opponents problems that they may not be able to solve. They are forced to start bidding at a high level and will often have difficulty finding their best fit and estimating their combined strength.

Preemptive bids are basically topsy-turvy, but somewhere among the madness normality returns: the more you bid, the longer and stronger your suit tends to be.

A basic guideline in preemptive bidding is the Rule of Two:

Number of cards in suit + two = number of tricks attempted

So if you bid two spades, trying for eight tricks, you normally have a six-card suit. If you bid three hearts, trying for nine tricks, you normally have a seven-card suit, and so on.

But as these are defensive bids, and you rather expect to fail unless partner has a good hand, you must resign yourself to the fact that now and again the opponents will double you and beat you a few tricks. This will be painful, especially if you are vulnerable.

So just as in making overcalls, which we discussed earlier, you must be more cautious when vulnerable. Consider these two hands as dealer:

a) ♠ 8 7
   ♥ K Q 8 7 4 3 2
   ♦ 5
   ♣ 6 4 3

b) ♠ 8 7
   ♥ K 8 7 5 4 3 2
   ♦ 5
   ♣ Q 7 3

Hand (a) is a good three-heart bid in any circumstances: you have a good chance of making six tricks even if partner is very weak. Hand (b) is more dangerous because the suit is weaker. If you are not vulnerable, bid three hearts anyway. Be aggressive. But if you are vulnerable the risk is too great. You should pass, fearing a heavy penalty.

Vulnerability and the strength of the suit are the most important factors influencing preemptive bids. But you should also consider your assets. There is always 1 long-suit asset, but there may or may not be short-suit assets. Consider these two hands:

a) ♠ —
   ♥ K Q J 10 7 6 3
   ♦ J 8 7 2
   ♣ 7 6

b) ♠ 8 3
   ♥ K Q J 10 7 6 3
   ♦ J 8
   ♣ 7 6

Both hands have strong seven-card suits and seem qualified for a three-heart bid. But (a) is obviously much better, counting two assets for the void spade.

If you are not vulnerable, hand (a) can bid a trick more than one would expect. Favorable vulnerability plus strong suit plus assets adds up to four hearts. Hand (b) bids a normal three hearts.

If you are vulnerable, hand (a) bids three hearts, the normal action. But hand (b) bids two hearts, giving the impression of a six-card suit. Even with a strong suit, unfavorable vulnerability and lack of assets dictate caution.

If your partner opens with a preemptive bid, responding presents special problems. High cards are useful, but the fit is vital. If your partner opens preemptively below game, count the number of cards in your partner's suit and: *with more than two-card support, tend to bid; with fewer than two-card support, tend to pass.* (With two-card support, no tendency.)

Suppose your partner opens three hearts, not vulnerable, and you hold:

a)		b)	
♠	3	♠	3
♡	A 9 6	♡	10 9 6
♢	A 7 6 4 3	♢	J 7 6 4 3
♣	K 10 5 2	♣	10 8 5 2

With (a), bid four hearts for two reasons.

The first reason is that you expect to make it. Imagine that your partner has one of the hands shown at the start of this section, with seven strong hearts and nothing else. He will succeed unless he loses three club tricks. That would be unlucky if he has three small clubs, and impossible if he has the queen.

The second reason is that you expect your opponents to make at least four spades. It is not certain, but it is quite likely that on defense you will make only the two red aces and one other trick.

Whenever there is a preemptive bid by your partner, think about what they can make as well as about what you can make.

With hand (b) opposite a three-heart bid it is obvious that you cannot make anything: you would expect three hearts to fail by two tricks.

But what can they make? Surely six spades, and perhaps seven spades, worth a large bonus. You have no defensive tricks, and it is not likely that your partner has any either. You should certainly bid four hearts, hoping to confuse matters for them, and if the opponents are vulnerable, and so headed for a bigger slam bonus, an imaginative player will bid five hearts or even six hearts. If doubled in his bid — called an **advance save** — he will go down 800 or 1100. But it will give the opponents a headache at a high level. They will not know whether to double or bid a slam. And if they decide to bid a slam they may not be sure which slam to bid.

This leads us to the problems of bidding over an opposing preempt. What do you do when your opponent opens preemptively at the two- or three-level and you have a good hand?

There is a simple guideline: *over a preempt, do as you would have done over a one-bid but more cautiously.*

Doubles are for takeout. Notrump overcalls resemble notrump opening bids, with something in the enemy suit. Suit overcalls show opening values and at least a good five-card suit.

Now back up a little, to the problem of responding to a preempt. Here are two hands, one of which we saw earlier:

a) ♠ 3
    ♡ A 9 6
    ◇ A 7 6 4 3
    ♣ K 10 5 2

b) ♠ 3
    ♡ K Q 5
    ◇ K Q 7 4
    ♣ K Q J 8 3

Before the opening bid was three hearts and you raised because you had a fit. But now the opening bid is three spades. What do you do? In each case you have good defense if the opponents choose to bid, so that is not a factor.

With hand (a) it is clear that you should pass. Your partner has, presumably, a good seven-card suit. It will be a struggle to make three spades let alone four.

Hand (a) does at least have two aces, providing two sure tricks. Hand (b) has no aces, and should also pass. Your 16 high-card points are unlikely to be enough for game opposite a hand containing nothing but a good seven-card suit: in four spades you must expect to lose at least one trump trick and three outside aces. Even three spades might go down. Queens and jacks in this situation are not worth much. Remember, with a misfit opposite a preemptive bid you tend to pass.

If hand (b) is strengthened a little by turning one of the kings into an ace the decision becomes closer. Once again, the vulnerability becomes a factor. You would bid four spades if vulnerable, but pass if not vulnerable.

This is just the same policy that applies in responding to an overcall. The partner of the overcaller and the preempter must be more aggressive when he is vulnerable because he knows that his partner is being cautious.

Notice when your partner makes a preemptive bid you should rarely think about playing in any contract except his suit. With hand (b) you should not consider three notrump, which is hardly ever the right move in this situation. You have a normal seven-one fit in his suit, and his hand will be virtually useless as a dummy. (The player who bids three practically never has a solid suit.)

The commonest preemptive bids are predictably at the two-level: two spades, two hearts, or two diamonds. These are weak two-bids, as distinct from the traditional strong two (see page 213).

Suppose that with both sides vulnerable you pick up this hand:

♠ K 7 6 4 2   ♡ A Q 9   ◇ Q 5   ♣ A 4 3

Your partner bids two hearts and the opponents are silent. What do you do?

You expect your partner to have a six-card heart suit and perhaps 8 high-card points. The range of his bid is usually 6-10. You are not afraid of any bidding by the opponents, and the only question is whether you can make four hearts. You have a nine-card fit, and the combined values seem almost sufficient.

You should not consider two spades, a forcing response that would suggest spades as a contract rather than hearts. And three hearts would be very wrong: that bid would show a weak hand, with no interest in game, that hopes to make life harder for the enemy. Partner would automatically pass that bid.

One possible bid would be two notrump. That is an exploring move that asks a question: is your weak two maximum or minimum?

Partner would rebid his suit with a minimum, or bid something else, usually a suit containing a high card, with a maximum.

But you decide to bid four hearts, for two reasons. First, you are vulnerable, the situation in which the opener's partner should be aggressive. Second, the bid may confuse the opponents a little. They cannot tell whether your four-heart bid is based on a weak hand with a fit, aiming to shut them out, or a strong hand in high cards on which you expect to make game.

The bidding ends, and as usual in this book you play the hand when you ought to be the dummy. Going round the table you see:

NORTH
♠ K 7 6 4 2
♡ A Q 9
◇ Q 5
♣ A 4 3

West leads the ♠Q

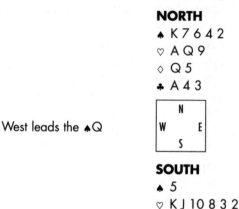

SOUTH
♠ 5
♡ K J 10 8 3 2
◇ A 6 3
♣ 10 8 6

The preliminary review is not encouraging. You seem to be on the way to losing four tricks, two clubs, a spade and a diamond, for down one. Unfortunately the lead makes it clear that East has the spade ace and that your king has no future. West would not lead the spade queen if he held the ace (that would be unwise in a suit contract).

If you count winners you will find nine: six trumps, two aces, and a diamond ruff in the dummy. Obviously the diamond ruff will have to be maneuvered before you draw trumps.

It would be foolish to play the spade king from dummy at the first trick: better a live dog than a dead lion. You play low from dummy, offering some hope that the king will score eventually. That could happen if East's ace is not well-guarded.

West's queen wins and, as you hoped, he perseveres with the spade jack. A shift to clubs would have been irritating.

You play low again from the dummy and ruff in your hand. Now you must hope that West has the king of diamonds. As it happens he does.

You lead a low diamond and if he plays low the queen wins. Then you can continue diamonds, ruffing one in the dummy, and the rest is easy. You will lose two clubs as well as the original spade trick.

But West puts up the diamond king and leads a club — too late. You win with the ace in dummy and play the diamond queen, winning a trick. Now you need the lead in your hand so you ruff a spade. To be on the safe side you ruff with the eight, and are glad you did when West discards a club.

The position is now this:

NORTH
♠ K 7
♡ A Q 9
♢ —
♣ 4 3

```
        N
    W       E
        S
```

SOUTH
♠ —
♡ K J 10 3
♢ A
♣ 10 8

Now your diamond maneuver shows a profit. You play the diamond ace and throw a club from the dummy. Now we have a potential ruff in clubs, because we have more clubs than dummy.

So lead a club. The opponents score a trick, but you are in control. You cannot be prevented from ruffing your remaining club and making the contract. You have eliminated one of your club losers.

The complete deal is:

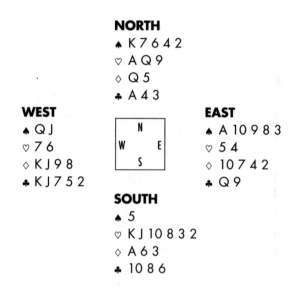

NORTH
♠ K 7 6 4 2
♡ A Q 9
◊ Q 5
♣ A 4 3

WEST
♠ Q J
♡ 7 6
◊ K J 9 8
♣ K J 7 5 2

EAST
♠ A 10 9 8 3
♡ 5 4
◊ 10 7 4 2
♣ Q 9

SOUTH
♠ 5
♡ K J 10 8 3 2
◊ A 6 3
♣ 10 8 6

This deal is a reminder of the most common reason for postponing trump leads: the ruff in the dummy. Some others are:

1. Taking a discard. If your opponents are threatening to take a trick in a side suit, look for a chance to score a winner in dummy. For example:

NORTH
♠ Q 10 8 3 2
♡ A K 4
◊ K 3 2
♣ A 3

SOUTH
♠ K J 9 7 6
♡ 7 6 2
◊ Q J
♣ 9 8 2

You are in four spades and the lead is the heart queen. You win in the dummy, and are in danger of losing a trick in each suit. If you play trumps the defenders will play another heart and you are dead.

Instead you must play diamonds at once. The enemy takes the diamond ace and plays another heart, which you win. Now cash the remaining diamond honor in your hand, cross to the club ace, and throw your heart loser on the diamond king. The defenders will score the spade ace and a club trick, and you are safe.

2. You plan ruffs in both hands, leaving the opponents' trumps at large permanently. This is a **crossruff**. If this is your plan, take any winners in other suits before doing the ruffing.

3. You plan to make use of a long suit in dummy but your eventual entry is in the trump suit. Establish the long suit first. For an example, see page 37.

QUIZ

1. Choose your opening bid as dealer with each of the following hands, assuming (i) you are vulnerable, opponents not; (ii) you are not vulnerable, opponents are.

   a) ♠ 8
   ♡ —
   ◇ A Q J 9 8 4 3 2
   ♣ J 10 9 4

   b) ♠ Q 9 7 6 4 3 2
   ♡ Q 5 2
   ◇ 5
   ♣ 8 6

2. Not vulnerable against vulnerable opponents, what would you respond to partner's opening two-spade bid, after a pass on your right, with each of the following hands?

   a) ♠ J
   ♡ A 6 2
   ◇ A K 8 3
   ♣ K Q 10 6 4

   b) ♠ K 8 7 2
   ♡ 5 3
   ◇ A 8 7 2
   ♣ Q 9 2

   c) ♠ —
   ♡ A 5 2
   ◇ A 7 2
   ♣ A K Q 8 7 3 2

3. Plan the play in four spades with the following layout:

NORTH
♠ K J 10 4
♡ Q 7 6 2
◇ 7
♣ A K J 3

SOUTH
♠ A Q 9 6
♡ 4
◇ A 9 8 4 2
♣ 8 7 2

West leads the heart king which wins the first trick, and then leads a trump.

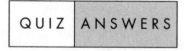

QUIZ ANSWERS

1. (a) (i) Four diamonds, the normal preemptive bid with a strong eight-card suit.
      (ii) Five diamonds, one more than normal, in view of the favorable vulnerability, the strong suit, and the extra assets.
   (b) (i) Pass. Vulnerable with a weak suit, three spades would be too risky.
      (ii) Three spades. With favorable vulnerability a weak suit is acceptable.

2. (a) Four spades. You are willing to play a six-one fit. If your partner has a good six-card suit he will probably make four spades. You have a good dummy for him, but his hand might be useless as a dummy in three notrump.
   (b) Four spades, expecting to go down a trick or two. But you are sure that the opponents can make four hearts and you must

make life hard for them. If they bid five hearts they might go
down.

(c) Three notrump. Whatever your partner has in spades you
should be able to take nine tricks: seven clubs and two aces.
Your partner should pass, since he has described his hand and
you are the captain.

3. Plan a crossruff, making as many tricks with trumps as possible.
But before you take the ruffs you must take your other winners.
Win the spade shift, take your three tricks in the minor suits, and
then ruff red cards, backward and forward, to score six more
tricks for a total of ten. If you do not cash the top clubs quickly,
they may be ruffed later.

ESSENTIALS TO REMEMBER

1. Preemptive opening suit bids, two diamonds and above, show
   long, strong suits lacking the high cards for a one-bid. Usually
   bid to a level requiring two tricks more than the number of cards
   in the suit. Take into account the strength of the suit, the vulnerability, and short-suit assets.

2. If partner opens preemptively, tend to raise regardless of
   strength, with a three-card fit or better; tend to pass, unless very
   strong indeed, with a misfit — a singleton or void in partner's
   suit.

3. If partner opens with a weak two-bid, a raise to three is weak. Bid
   two notrump to probe: opener rebids his suit with a minimum.

4. In a suit contract, look for reasons to postpone trump leads. The
   usual reason is the need to ruff in dummy. Others are the crossruff (cash side winners early and never draw trumps), the need
   for a quick discard, or the need for a trump entry to dummy after
   establishing dummy's suit.

Sooner or later, in any bridge game, there will be a partnership mud-dle leading to a sad postmortem: 'I thought it was forcing' or 'I didn't think it was forcing'.

It is vitally important to be sure you can distinguish between forcing and non-forcing natural bids. (Obviously artificial bids such as Blackwood and Stayman are forcing.) If you cannot, your sad post-mortems will be far too frequent.

Using the modern style (but see page 213) there is a general rule: *nothing is forcing except a new suit by the opener's partner.* Here are some forcing situations that follow the general rule:

a) **North**	**South**	b) **North**	**South**	c) **North**	**South**
1♡	1♠	1♡	2♣	1♡	2♠

d) **North**	**South**	e) **North**	**South**	f) **North**	**South**
1♡	1♠	3◊	3♠	1♡	1♠
2♡	3♣			2◊	3♣

Bidding sequence (f) is a 'Fourth-Suit' bid (see page 214). There is one exceptional forcing bid by the responder (that is, opener's part-ner):

g)	**North**	**South**
	1♡	2NT

As South shows the values for an opening bid, and two opening bids add up to game, the situation is clearly forcing.

There are two situations, rather obvious ones, in which the new suit by the opener's partner is not forcing:

1. When the previous bid was one notrump, making partner the captain with the right to make decisions:

h)	**North**	**South**	i)	**North**	**South**
	1NT	2♡		1♣	1♠
				1NT	2♡

In (h), two hearts shows a weak hand and ends the bidding[1].

In (i) South is not interested in game opposite his partner's balanced hand in the 13-14 point range. North is asked to choose between the major suits: he passes if he is longer in hearts, and otherwise gives preference to spades. Always give preference to partner's first suit, which may be longer, when you like the suits equally.

2.   When opener's partner (the responder) has already passed:

i)	**North**	**South**		k)	**North**	**South**
	pass	1♡			pass	1♡
	1♠				2◇	

The passed-hand bid is not forcing because the bidder has already denied the 13 points needed for an opening. If the opener has a minimum he can tell that the combined point count is less than 26. But the opener will bid again if he has more than a minimum (see 'Third Seat,' page 204, and 'Fourth Seat,' page 204).

Most forcing bids show good hands on which you expect to reach game. However, the most common forcing bid is an exception. Sequence (a) above (one heart-one spade) and similar suit responses at the one-level may be based on very weak hands with just 6 points. Of course, they may also represent strong hands on which game is likely or certain.

Consider these two sequences:

l)	**North**	**South**		m)	**North**	**South**
	1♡	2♠			1♣	1♡
					2♠	

These are rather rare and are a special category: the jump in a new suit, or **jump shift**.

These always guarantee game, for otherwise there would be no need to skip a level. Sequence (l) suggests a slam. Sequence (m), a jump shift by the opener, is almost the only clear exception to the

---

1. In the modern style, however, two hearts would be a transfer showing spade length.

general rule: it is a natural forcing bid by the opener. If the opener bids a new suit without a jump (one club-one heart-one spade) it is not forcing[2]. The opener can make a forcing bid in a new suit after a raise (1♠–2♠; 3◊, or 1♠-3♠; 4◊) but these bids are really artificial: there is not the slightest intention of playing in diamonds.

There are, however, two situations in which the opener's natural rebid has a forcing flavor:

n)	**North**	**South**	o)	**North**	**South**
	1♠	2♣		1♣	1♡
	2◊			2NT	

In (n) North can have a minimum hand. But since South has shown a good hand (normally 10 or more high-card points) he always bids again.

In (o) South has promised 6 points or more and the opener 18-20. The combined hands are close to the 26-point mark and the bidding hardly ever dies.

We can now restate the general rule, with a little more precision, the other way round.

Natural bids are not forcing unless they are:

1) *a new suit by responder who did not pass originally (and not even then following one notrump) or*

2) *a jump in a new suit by either player or an immediate jump to two notrump by responder.*

Suppose that your partner bids one heart and as North you have:

♠ A 8 6 5   ♡ K Q 6   ◊ Q 7 2   ♣ 5 4 2

You expect to play in hearts, since there is sure to be at least an eight-card fit, but you should start by probing with one spade. Partner rebids two clubs and you should jump to three hearts.

---

2. Some reverse sequences are forcing, e.g.: 1♡-2♣; 2♠. Opener is showing 17+ and responder has promised 10+, so clearly the partnership wants to get to game. However, for the purpose of creating a 'general rule', we're going to ignore these auctions.

Two hearts would be weak, suggesting a final contract. Three hearts is a secondary jump, inviting game. In accordance with the rules above, the bid is not forcing (but see page 213).

The result will usually be a four-heart bid from partner, ending the auction. Occasionally your partner will pass three hearts, with a dead minimum opening, and occasionally he will move toward slam. In this case your partner is feeling aggressive. He bids four notrump, a Blackwood bid asking for aces. You bid five diamonds, showing one, and he bids six hearts.

As usual, you move around the table to play the hand for your partner and see this:

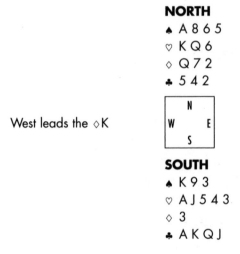

NORTH

♠ A 8 6 5
♡ K Q 6
◇ Q 7 2
♣ 5 4 2

West leads the ◇K

SOUTH

♠ K 9 3
♡ A J 5 4 3
◇ 3
♣ A K Q J

South has 18 high-card points and 2 assets. Since North's invitational jump suggested about 11 points, and there was only an eight-card fit, South should not have been so ambitious. He could not count 33 points in the combined hands, but he was encouraged by his partial fit in spades.

Now we have to find a way to make twelve tricks when there seem to be only eleven: five hearts, four clubs, and two spades. One chance is that West will follow his diamond king by leading the ace. That would set up the queen in dummy as a trick, but unfortunately West does not fall into the trap: he shifts to a trump.

When, as here, you have almost enough tricks and have lost all that you can afford to lose, there may be scope for some bridge magic.

Put off the evil day as long as possible by leading out winners. But make sure that you keep communication between the two hands. In this case, take all the trumps and all the clubs. After nine tricks, with one club winner remaining, the position happens to be:

NORTH
♠ A 8 6
♡ —
◊ Q
♣ —

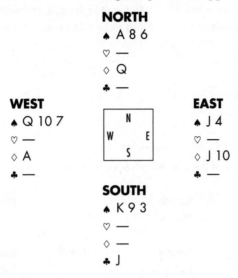

WEST
♠ Q 10 7
♡ —
◊ A
♣ —

EAST
♠ J 4
♡ —
◊ J 10
♣ —

SOUTH
♠ K 9 3
♡ —
◊ —
♣ J

Lead the club jack, and ruin West. He must either throw the diamond ace, allowing the queen to make later in dummy, or throw a spade, allowing South to make his twelfth trick in that suit.

The complete deal was:

NORTH
♠ A 8 6 5
♡ K Q 6
◊ Q 7 2
♣ 5 4 2

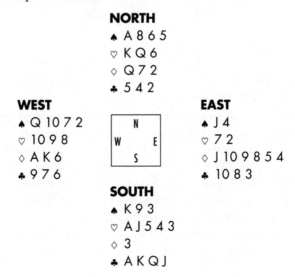

WEST
♠ Q 10 7 2
♡ 10 9 8
◊ A K 6
♣ 9 7 6

EAST
♠ J 4
♡ 7 2
◊ J 10 9 8 5 4
♣ 10 8 3

SOUTH
♠ K 9 3
♡ A J 5 4 3
◊ 3
♣ A K Q J

This was a **squeeze**, an advanced play technique with many ramifications beyond the scope of this book. But there are a few guidelines to remember: (1) lose quickly any tricks that must be lost; (2) look for situations that may be a problem for the defense, in this case the diamond queen and the spade length (these are called **menaces** or **threats**); (3) lead out sure winners, preserving communications.

QUIZ

---

1. Look at each of the following sequences. Is the last bid forcing?

   a) | **North** | **South** |
      |---|---|
      | 1♡ | 3♡ |

   b) | **North** | **South** |
      |---|---|
      | 1♡ | 1♠ |

   c) | **North** | **South** |
      |---|---|
      | 1♡ | 1♠ |
      | 2♣ | |

   d) | **North** | **South** |
      |---|---|
      | 1♡ | 1♠ |
      | 2♣ | 2♡ |

   e) | **North** | **South** |
      |---|---|
      | 1♡ | 1♠ |
      | 2♣ | 3♠ |

   f) | **North** | **South** |
      |---|---|
      | 1♡ | 2♡ |
      | 3♢ | |

   g) | **North** | **South** |
      |---|---|
      | 1♣ | 1♠ |
      | 1NT | 2♡ |

2. Review the sequences in Question 1. How many points do you expect in the hand of the player making the last bid?

3. Plan the play as South in six notrump with the following hands:

NORTH
♠ 6 5 2
♡ Q 8 7
♦ 7 2
♣ A K Q 6 4

SOUTH
♠ A J 4 3
♡ A K J 2
♦ A K Q
♣ 5 2

The bidding was: two notrump-six notrump. West leads the spade king.

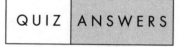

1. (a) Not forcing, an invitation, because the suit has been bid.
   (b) Forcing, a new suit by responder.
   (c) Not forcing. (A new suit by the opener is not forcing.)
   (d) Forcing, a new suit by responder (see page 213).
   (e) Not forcing, the suit has been bid already.
   (f) Forcing. Since we have found a heart fit, we cannot want to play diamonds. This shows some diamonds, but has an artificial quality.
   (g) Not forcing, because it follows a one notrump bid.

2. (a) Expect 10-12, including assets.
   (b) Expect 6 or more; no upper limit.
   (c) Expect 13-19 including assets; probably 11-18 in high cards.
   (d) Expect 10 or more; no upper limit (for some it is 12 or more and game-forcing).
   (e) Expect 10-12 including assets.

(f) Probably 17-19 including assets; enough to invite game when partner has 6-10.

(g) Expect 6-9; an attempt to play two spades or two hearts rather than one notrump.

3. You can count eleven tricks, and the club suit offers an obvious chance of a twelfth. If you try that play at once you are putting all your eggs in one basket. There is only about one chance in three that the six clubs in the opponents' hands will be divided three-three.

Squeeze play improves your chances. You are willing to lose a trick, so lose it immediately: allow the spade king to win the first trick. You will be happy if West leads another spade but let us suppose he shifts to the club jack.

You know that West has the spade queen, to justify his original king lead. If he also has most of the missing clubs he will be in trouble. You take your diamond winners, your spade ace and three heart tricks to reach this position:

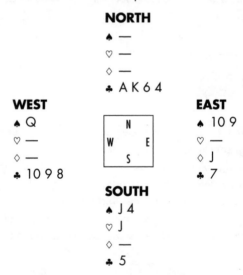

NORTH
♠ —
♡ —
◇ —
♣ A K 6 4

WEST
♠ Q
♡ —
◇ —
♣ 10 9 8

EAST
♠ 10 9
♡ —
◇ J
♣ 7

SOUTH
♠ J 4
♡ J
◇ —
♣ 5

As planned, the lead of the heart jack destroys West. However he chooses to discard, declarer will make his twelfth trick in one of the black suits.

We began with threats in the black suits. We conceded the trick we had to lose. And we cashed winners, keeping our link to the clubs in the North hand.

ESSENTIALS TO REMEMBER

1. Natural bids (that is, excluding conventions and bids made when a trump suit has been found) are only forcing if they are new-suit bids by opener's partner or a new-suit jump by opener. Exception: a minimum new-suit bid is not forcing when it follows one notrump, and some reverses by opener are forcing.

2. If you are short a trick, a squeeze may be the solution. Try to lose quickly the tricks you can afford to lose. Keep intact cards that may threaten an opponent. And make sure that at the finish you can cross from one hand to the other.

The reader is now accustomed to the simple methods of valuation described at the beginning of this book: count high-card points, add assets, and revise the assets according to the degree of fit. But there are a few more advanced aspects that have to be taken into account.

One thing to remember is that aces are actually worth a little more than four points. And tens are also useful, although not given a value. You can think of these two factors together and follow this guideline: *bid cautiously if short of aces and tens, bid aggressively with several aces and tens.*

The quantity of points is not the whole story, either: they can be in the right place or the wrong place. Consider these two opening hands:

a) ♠ K Q 4 3 2   b) ♠ K 5 4 3 2
♡ A J 4 3 2   ♡ J 5 4 3 2
◊ A 2   ◊ A Q
♣ 2   ♣ A

Hand (a) is much better than hand (b) because most of the high-card points are in the long suits.

When in doubt, be aggressive when most of the high cards are in the long suits. Be cautious when they are mostly in the short suits.

The same is true if the bidding shows that your partner has one long suit or two long suits. High cards in his suits are golden. Consider this situation:

NORTH   **SOUTH**
1♠   1NT
2♡

North's bidding is not encouraging. The usual result is a contract of two hearts or two spades. South frequently passes, when his hearts are longer than his spades, or makes a preference bid of two spades.

♠ 7 5   ♡ 9 8 3 2   ◇ K Q 4 2   ♣ K J 5

With this hand South passes two hearts. His hand will not be a useful dummy because he has no high cards in his partner's suits.

♠ K 5   ♡ A J 7 2   ◇ 9 8 3 2   ♣ 8 7 2

This hand, with one high-card point fewer, is the direct opposite, with all its high cards in the right place, in partner's suits. South should certainly support hearts, and an expert might choose to raise to four hearts rather than three.

Back from theory to practice. It is your bid with this hand:

♠ 4 2   ♡ A 10 3   ◇ K 9 8   ♣ K Q J 9 8

Obviously you bid one club, and your partner responds one diamond. What now?

A direct raise of a minor suit shows four-card support, so you cannot bid two diamonds. Two clubs would break the Golden Rule: you must have six cards to rebid your original suit. That leaves one notrump, not ideal with such weak spades but certainly the least evil.

Your partner bids two notrump, inviting game, and you must decide whether you do or do not have a minimum opening. Remember, your rebid showed 13-14 points, enough to open in a suit but not enough to open one notrump.

Counting your five-card suit as an asset you have 14 points. You have one ace and one ten, which is about average. But you should be aggressive and bid three notrump because 6 of your points are in clubs: it is an advantage to have high cards in long suits.

You are expecting a spade lead, but West leads a heart. You are now looking at:

NORTH

♠ A Q 8
♡ Q 6
◊ 7 5 4 2
♣ A 4 3 2

West leads the heart four

SOUTH

♠ 4 2
♡ A 10 3
◊ K 9 8
♣ K Q J 9 8

You can count seven sure tricks: five clubs and two aces. Two more are needed, and one of them will come from the heart suit if you play correctly to the first trick. If you did not have the ten it would be right to play the queen. As it is, however, that would be a serious error: if East produced the king you might take only one trick in the suit.

It is clearly right to play low. To prevent your scoring the ten East will have to play an honor, and you will win with the ace. A second trick is guaranteed, sooner or later, with the queen or the ten.

So you play low, East puts up the king, and you win with the ace. Now you have eight tricks, and there are two chances for the ninth. If West has the spade king you can finesse the queen successfully. If East has the diamond ace you can lead toward your king with a good result.

So what do you do first? Do not consider postponing the issue by playing clubs. Such plays are nearly always wrong: fast tricks should be played slowly. Whether you should start with spades or diamonds is the sixty-four-thousand-dollar question. Make up your mind.

If you play one and it fails, you want to be able to fall back on the other. The solution, therefore, is to go for diamonds. At the second trick, cross to dummy with a club to the ace and lead a diamond. East is likely to play low (playing the ace would help you) and you try the king. If it wins you have nine tricks. If not you are almost certain to have a chance to take the spade finesse later.

It is quite wrong to start with the spade finesse, for if that loses you are unlikely to have a second chance. The defense will clear hearts (or even spades) and it will be too late to score the diamond king.

The problem you faced at the first trick is a common one. With a doubleton queen or doubleton jack in the suit led and some strength in your hand, should you play dummy's honor?

Here are some examples of queen situations. The contract is three notrump, and in each case West has led the heart three.

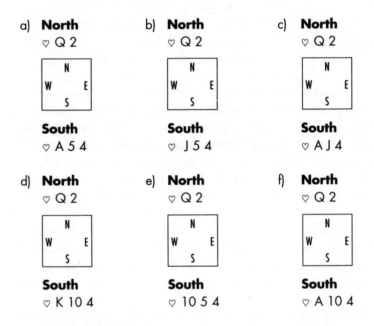

a) **North**
♡ Q 2

```
      N
  W       E
      S
```

South
♡ A 5 4

b) **North**
♡ Q 2

```
      N
  W       E
      S
```

South
♡ J 5 4

c) **North**
♡ Q 2

```
      N
  W       E
      S
```

South
♡ A J 4

d) **North**
♡ Q 2

```
      N
  W       E
      S
```

South
♡ K 10 4

e) **North**
♡ Q 2

```
      N
  W       E
      S
```

South
♡ 10 5 4

f) **North**
♡ Q 2

```
      N
  W       E
      S
```

South
♡ A 10 4

In case (a) you must obviously try the queen in the hope that the king is on your left. If it is on your right the queen will be captured sooner or later.

In case (b) you are sure of a trick eventually if you play low. Playing the queen will often leave you trickless.

Case (c) is less obvious. You are likely to make exactly two tricks whatever you do, but you should play the queen. If this wins, your ace-jack will prevent the hand on your left from leading the suit again. If your right-hand opponent has the king he will play it on the queen sooner or later whatever you do.

Case (d) is easy. Play low from dummy to be sure of two tricks.

Case (e) is almost hopeless, but you should try the queen from dummy in the faint hope that West has led from ace-king.

Case (f) was discussed above. Play low to guarantee two tricks.

It is not necessary to memorize these situations, or the others like them. You can, if you wish, work them out as they arise at the table, but there is a general guideline.

Count the number of *significant* high cards owned by the opposition:

Case (a) one, the king; case (c) one, the king; case (e) three, ace, king, and jack. Play high from dummy.

Case (b) two, the ace and king; case (d) two, the ace and jack; case (f) two, king and jack. Play low from dummy.

We can now state the guideline: *if the opponents have two significant cards, play low. Otherwise play high.* With rare exceptions, this works whenever dummy has a doubleton queen or a doubleton jack. Test this for yourself. More examples are below, in the quiz section.

QUIZ

1. As dealer, which of the following hands would you rather have, and why?

    a) ♠ A K
       ♡ Q 7 6 3 2
       ◇ K 7 6 3 2
       ♣ 2

    b) ♠ 5 2
       ♡ A Q 10 3 2
       ◇ A J 10 3 2
       ♣ 2

2. If your partner opened one spade, which of the following hands would you rather have, and why?

    a) ♠ Q 10 6 2
       ♡ 10 9 6 2
       ◇ 4 3 2
       ♣ A 3

    b) ♠ 7 6 3 2
       ♡ Q J 5 2
       ◇ Q 3 2
       ♣ Q J

3. You are in three notrump, the lead is the two of spades, and
    dummy has a doubleton, the jack and three. What should you
    play from dummy if the spade holding in your hand is:

    a) ♠ A K 4   b) ♠ A 10 4   c) ♠ A 9 4
    d) ♠ Q 5 4   e) ♠ A Q 4   f) ♠ K Q 9 4

QUIZ	ANSWERS

1. The hands have the same distribution and the same assets. Hand
    (a) has 12 high-card points and (b) 11, but nevertheless hand (b)
    is slightly better. In the ace-and-ten department, (b) outnumbers (a)
    four to one. Also (b) has all its points in the long suits while (a) has
    the majority in the short suits.

2. The distribution and assets are the same, and (b) has two more
    high-card points. Nevertheless, (a) is preferable since all the
    points are 'working': the spade queen is sure to be useful to part-
    ner, and an ace is always useful. Also you have two tens. Hand
    (b) has no aces or tens, and the points are in the wrong places.
    At least one of the queens is sure to be useless.

3. Play low if, and only if, the opponents have two significant cards.
    (a) Play the jack, hoping the queen, the only significant card the
        opponents have, is on the left.
    (b) Play low, guaranteeing two tricks. The opponents have two
        cards that matter, the king and queen.
    (c) Play the jack. The opponents have three significant cards, king,
        queen, and ten. The only slight hope of making two tricks is
        that the leader has the king and the queen.
    (d) Play low to guarantee one trick. The opponents have two cards
        of importance, the ace and the king.
    (e) The opponents have one important card, the king. Play the
        jack, so that if it wins you are protected against another lead
        of the suit from your left. If you play low and East has the king
        he will save it for the next round of the suit.
    (f) Play low to make sure of three tricks. The opponents have two
        significant cards, the ace and ten.

ESSENTIALS TO REMEMBER

1. In close situations be aggressive if you have (a) aces and tens, (b) high cards in your suits, (c) high cards in your partner's suits.

2. If dummy has a doubleton queen or jack in the suit led, play low if the opponents have two significant cards. Otherwise play high.

3. If you have two ways to try for an extra trick, select the one that will permit you, if necessary, to fall back on the other.

As we saw in yesterday's chapter, a bidder's prospects change when he considers what his partner has shown. Honors in his suits will be valuable, honors in other suits, especially queens and jacks, are of uncertain worth. Other activity, or inactivity, must be taken into account.

RIGHT-HAND OPPONENT

If there is a suit bid on your right, whether an opening bid or an overcall, inspect your holding in that suit.

Suppose you have a doubleton king in the enemy suit. It is now highly probable that the ace is on your right. The king is almost sure to be worth a trick, and is virtually the equivalent of an ace. If you have the ace-queen of the enemy suit, expect to take two tricks because the king should be on your right.

Conversely, you should be worried if you have, say, three small cards. The opponents are likely to take two or three tricks in the suit, for any honor cards in your partner's hand will be in jeopardy.

If your right-hand opponent bids, strength in that suit becomes stronger and weakness becomes weaker.

LEFT-HAND OPPONENT

This is the other side of the coin. If your left-hand opponent bids, inspect your holding in that suit. A king is now of dubious value, for it will probably be captured by the enemy ace. An ace-queen will be useful if you are declarer and the suit is led, but otherwise the queen can be expected to lose to the king.

Weakness in the enemy suit is not good, but there are two silver linings: any strength your partner may have in the suit is well-placed, and your honor cards in other suits will pull their weight.

If your left-hand opponent bids, strength in that suit becomes weaker.

THIRD SEAT

If you have the chance to open the bidding in third seat, following passes by your partner and your right-hand opponent, you can relax your standards slightly. An opening bid can be a fraction weaker, by a point or two. With a minimum hand the five-card major requirement can be relaxed: bid a strong four-card major and plan to pass any bid by your partner.

Your partner will have this in mind when responding to your bid. He will have at least five-card length to bid a new suit at the two-level, and he will often raise, perhaps even jump to the three-level, with three-card support.

The reason is this: if you have a minimum and your partner could not open you are unlikely to have a game. The strongest hand at the table is probably on your left, and the enemy may bid a game. If you bid a strong suit with a weak hand you may help your partner to find the best opening lead.

The same third-seat policy applies to preemptive bids, a three-bid or a weak two. Relax the requirements a little, if not vulnerable, by venturing a three-bid with a good six-card suit or a weak two-bid with a good five-card suit.

FOURTH SEAT

This is rather different. If all the other players have passed you can end the bidding with a fourth pass. If you have 10 high-card points, an average hand, the odds are that all the players have something similar.

With 11 or 12 points you may venture to open in the hope of a partscore. It is unlikely that anyone can make game. But observe this guideline: for a borderline opening you must have length in spades — at least three cards and preferably more. If you are short in spades there is a serious danger that the opponents will start bidding that suit and outbid you.

Now from theory to practice. As South you deal yourself this:

♠ K J 5 4   ♡ K 5   ◇ Q J 10   ♣ 9 8 7 6

The bidding starts:

West	North	East	South
	(partner)		(you)
			pass
pass	1 ♡	1 ♠	??

You should not consider a double, for it hardly ever pays to try for a penalty at the one-level. (And the double may mean something else — see page 205.)

Prospects look good in notrump, and particularly good in view of the spade holding. East is quite likely to have the ace-queen of spades to justify his overcall, so your king-jack is very strong. You are likely to take two spade tricks, and should jump to two notrump.

In other circumstances this jump to two notrump would be forcing, showing values for an opening bid (an exception to the general rule: see page 185). But here you denied opening values when you passed originally.

Your partner will expect you to have some spade strength, to prevent East taking a lot of spade tricks, and close to an opening bid. He will presume 11 or 12 points, but your 10 is certainly worth 11 because of the upgraded spade strength.

Your partner continues to three notrump, ending the bidding. When he puts down his dummy you see:

NORTH
♠ 6 2
♡ A J 10 9 8
◊ A 9 4 2
♣ A 10

West leads the ♠8

SOUTH
♠ K J 5 4
♡ K 5
◊ Q J 10
♣ 9 8 7 6

You play low from dummy, East plays low, and you win with the jack. You infer that East has the ace-queen and is saving his ace temporarily.

Count your tricks. You expect to make a second spade trick, and one trick is the limit in clubs. You need six tricks from the red suits, and there are three in clear view.

If you lose a trick in either red suit the defenders will persevere with spades, removing your king. At that point you will be in some jeopardy. Let's look at both possible plans — hearts first and diamonds first.

If you play hearts and lose a trick to the queen, you will have eight tricks. For the ninth you will have to try the diamond finesse. If it loses — as is likely since East entered the bidding — you will be defeated. Your opponents will have taken three spade tricks and a trick in each red suit.

Playing diamonds is a better proposition. If the finesse wins you are safe, but then you would have been safe with any play. Assume it loses to the king and that East cashes the spade ace. He then leads the queen and you win with the king. West throws a club, you throw a club from dummy and you are now in this position:

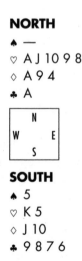

NORTH
♠ —
♡ A J 10 9 8
◇ A 9 4
♣ A

```
      N
  W       E
      S
```

SOUTH
♠ 5
♡ K 5
◇ J 10
♣ 9 8 7 6

You have one very useful piece of information: East has two more spades, which will score tricks if he gets the lead, but West has none. We can therefore follow the plan of play we discussed on page 168: **avoidance**. We can maneuver so that if we lose a trick it will be to West.

We might as well take our diamond tricks now, because we want to have the lead in the dummy. So lead the diamond jack and follow with the ten. Overtake with the ace and lead the nine, throwing a club.

Now the stage is set: lead the heart-jack and play low unless East covers with the queen. If West wins with the queen he cannot hurt you and you take the rest of the tricks, giving you one more than you need. If the jack wins, you lead to the king in your hand, return to the ace of clubs in dummy and make at least nine tricks.

The complete deal was:

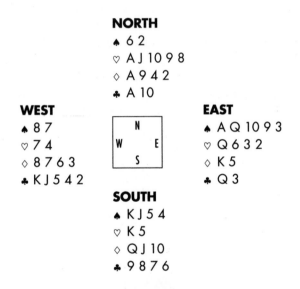

NORTH
♠ 6 2
♡ A J 10 9 8
◇ A 9 4 2
♣ A 10

WEST
♠ 8 7
♡ 7 4
◇ 8 7 6 3
♣ K J 5 4 2

EAST
♠ A Q 10 9 3
♡ Q 6 3 2
◇ K 5
♣ Q 3

SOUTH
♠ K J 5 4
♡ K 5
◇ Q J 10
♣ 9 8 7 6

On this deal South had a clue to the location of the spade honors: East had bid the suit. He had a clue to the diamond king: East's bid suggested some general strength. There was a slight clue to the location of the heart queen: again, East's bid.

When you are planning the play, any clues to the location of the enemy high cards are welcome. There are three common types of inference:

1. *High cards.* Think how many high-card points each of your opponents showed by bidding, or by not bidding. Then count how many points he has shown in the play.

Suppose an opponent passed his partner's opening bid. He would have responded with 6 points or more. If he produces an ace or a king you can be sure that he has little or nothing else.

If a player has shown the values for an opening bid, watch his high cards. If he does not produce much, then he probably has any important card that you are worrying about.

If neither opponent bids there may not seem to be any clues. You should usually assume that the missing high-card strength is divided about equally: if one player held it all he might have entered the bidding.

2. *Length.* If you know from the bidding or play that one opponent has a long suit the information can be helpful. Most of the unknown cards in the other suits will be in the other hand. Here is a simple example. Your contract is four hearts and West has led the spade jack.

NORTH
♠ Q 5 2
♡ K J 9 6
◊ 7 2
♣ A 8 4 3

SOUTH
♠ A 7 4
♡ A 10 8 5
◊ A Q J 10
♣ 10 7

There is no hurry to play the spade queen from dummy so you play low. A funny thing happens: East plays the king.

You win with the ace, happily, and must decide how to play the trumps. Playing the ace and king is in general wrong (although it might be right in special circumstances). The queen is likely to be guarded more than once, as we have seen before, so you must decide which way to finesse. Who has the queen?

You cannot be sure, but East on your right is a strong favorite. It is clear that he began with one spade, for he would not have wasted his king if he could help it. So West began with six spades, and has seven unknown cards. East began with one spade, and has twelve unknown cards.

The odds are twelve to seven, or almost two to one, that East has the heart queen. So you lead to the heart king in dummy, play the jack, and finesse with modest confidence if East plays low.

3. *Distribution.* All bridge hands have a **distribution**, or pattern, indicating the length of the suits. The hands shown just above have the most common pattern, four-four-three-two. (The longest suit is shown first and the shortest last unless you wish to emphasize the length of specific suits. The two hands above could be described as (North) three-four-two-four and (South) three-four-four-two.)

These are the eleven most common distributions, and should become old friends. Look for them when you pick up your hand, or when the dummy appears. If you make this a habit you will know immediately if somebody deals you twelve or fourteen cards in error.

Balanced	4-4-3-2	5-3-3-2	4-3-3-3		
One-suiter	6-3-2-2	6-3-3-1	7-3-2-1		
Two-suiter	5-4-3-1	5-4-2-2	6-4-2-1	5-5-2-1	6-4-3-0
Three-suiter	4-4-4-1	5-4-4-0			

Awareness of these distribution patterns helps in three ways:

1. If you are an inexperienced player, this helps you to remember how things were at the start. You can mentally reconstruct your own hand or the dummy quite easily if you recall the distribution.

2. The pattern of a hand is also the pattern of a suit: a way of dividing thirteen cards into four groups. When you are used to the pattern you have less counting to do.

   Suppose that you have a four-four fit and that an opponent shows out on the second round. That player had one card, and you will know that the other opponent began with four cards if you think of the four-four-four-one pattern. When three elements in the puzzle are known, the fourth falls into place.

3. For the more experienced player there is a big bonus. After a time it becomes possible to count the distribution of an unseen hand. If you know three suits, the fourth element in the pattern slots into place.

   Against three notrump an opponent leads the two of diamonds. Later you discover that he had only one club. You can be fairly sure that his pattern was four-four-four-one. His fourth-best lead indicated a four-card suit, and he would no doubt have led from a five-card suit if one had been available.

Q U I Z

1. You are defending three notrump and your club suit consists of ace-queen-ten-eight. Estimate your defensive chances if the clubs were bid (a) on your right; (b) on your left.

2. You have this hand:

   ♠ 4 2   ♡ K Q 10 5   ◊ K J 7 2   ♣ K 8 7

   What would you do: (a) as dealer? (b) in third seat after two passes? (c) in fourth seat after three passes?

3. You are East, defending three notrump:

NORTH
♠ A 5 4 2
♡ Q 7 6 3
♢ A 5 4
♣ 6 2

EAST
♠ J 10 8 7 3
♡ J 5
♢ 8 7
♣ J 10 8 7

West	North	East	South
			1NT
pass	2♣	pass	2♢
pass	3NT	all pass	

Your partner leads the king of diamonds and continues the suit. South holds up dummy's ace as long as he can. On the third round, as dummy wins the ace, you throw a spade and so does South.

What is South's distribution?

QUIZ ANSWERS

1. (a) Your prospects are excellent, with the suit bid on the right. There is a good chance that the bidder has king-jack-nine, and will be unhappy when you destroy each of those cards in turn.
    (b) Your prospects are poor, with the suit bid on the left. You will be lucky to take more than one trick in the suit, and the bidder will probably score the king and the jack.

2. (a) Pass. You do not quite have the 13 points needed for an opening bid.

(b) Bid one heart. In third seat you can be slightly flexible, and you try to bid a strong suit that you would like your partner to lead. The five-card major rule does not apply here.

(c) Pass. There is a temptation to bid, but there is a danger that the opponents will find a fit in spades. If the hearts were spades, you could bid one spade.

3. Think about the bidding. Two clubs was Stayman, asking South to bid a major suit. Two diamonds denied having one.

The early play showed that South began with two diamonds. So what distribution can he have?

Answer: five-three-three-two, or specifically three-three-two-five (3-3 in the majors with a five-card club suit). South has a concealed five-card club suit, and as East you had better hang on to all your clubs. They will be important.

ESSENTIALS TO REMEMBER

1. Honor cards improve in value if the right-hand opponent bids the suit, but lose value if the suit is bid to the left.

2. After two passes, open with a point or two below normal values. Do the same after three passes provided you have at least three spades.

3. In planning the play, think about clues to the length and strength of each opponent's hand.

STYLES & CONVENTIONS

The bidding in this book is based on the style that has long been standard in clubs and tournaments. However, the majority of social players still use the traditional methods that were popular half a century ago. Trouble can ensue when a modern tournament player faces a social traditionalist. There must be some meeting of the minds.

If you play with someone you do not know, it is vital to discuss the style of bidding you will use.

Two-bids. The modern player uses the weak two-bid combined with the strong artificial two clubs bid, as described in Day 17 and Day 18. The traditionalist prefers the strong two-bid: any opening two-bid in a suit is natural, is forcing, and guarantees game. The negative response is two notrump.

Responder's jumps. In the modern style, jump bids by the responder are invitational (exceptions: two notrump response to one of a suit and a jump in an unbid suit). Traditionally, all these bids are forcing. Compromises are possible, but need careful discussion (see 'Strong Raise' below).

Scientific style. Many tournament players use a bidding style that includes two special elements that work in combination. 1) Suit responses at the two-level such as one spade-two diamonds guarantee a game unless the responder rebids his suit. 2) A one-notrump response to a major-suit opening is treated as forcing, and includes many hands in the 10-12-point range. The opening bidder is often forced to bid a three-card minor suit after the forcing one-notrump response.

☐

The following advanced points, mainly artificial conventions, are for those who wish to take part in club play and tournaments. In alphabetical order:

Drury. Two clubs in response to a third-seat or fourth-seat bid of one heart or one spade can be artificial. By agreement, it shows at least 3 cards in opener's suit and 9-12 points. Opener rejects the game suggestion by rebidding his suit.

Flannery. An artificial two-diamonds opening promising exactly four spades, exactly five hearts, and 11-15 high-card points. A two-notrump response asks for a further description.

Fourth suit. If the first three bids by the partnership are in different suits, the responder often has a problem. For example:

♠ A J 6 5 2   ♡ 6 4 3   ◇ A 5   ♣ K J 6

Opener	Responder
1◇	1♠
2♣	??

The responder wishes to play game, but anything except hearts might be right. The solution is to make the 'fourth-suit' bid of two hearts, a waiting move. This announces game interest but says nothing about hearts: the opener must have a heart stopper to bid notrump. For many a fourth-suit bid is game-forcing.

Gambling three notrump. Since very strong hands all open two clubs, three notrump (traditionally 25-27 points) is relatively useless as an opening bid. The modern meaning is a very long (seven or more cards), solid minor suit with little else. Partner passes with moderate strength, or escapes by bidding clubs at whatever level he chooses, allowing the opener to correct to diamonds if necessary.

Gerber. A jump from one notrump or two notrump to four clubs, asking for aces on the Blackwood principle. Four diamonds shows no ace (or four), four hearts shows one, and so on.

Jacoby two notrump. A response of two notrump to one heart or one spade normally shows a balanced hand with 13-15 points and stoppers in the unbid suits. By agreement, it can show a strong hand and a fit with opener's suit. Opener must bid a singleton or void if he can. Failing that, he jumps to game with a minimum.

Landy. An artificial bid of two clubs following an opposing one-notrump bid. It shows overcalling values with length in spades and hearts.

Lebensohl. When one notrump is overcalled, responder can use two notrump, by agreement, to force three clubs. For example:

West	North	East	South
1NT	2♡	2NT	pass
3♣	pass	3♢	

This shows a weak hand with a long diamond suit. A direct three-diamond bid would be forcing.

Michaels. An immediate cuebid in the enemy suit (two diamonds over one diamond, or two spades over one spade) shows a two-suiter. If the opening bid is in a minor the Michaels bidder has at least five cards in each major suit. After a major-suit opening the cuebid shows the other major and one of the minors. Partner can bid two notrump to ask 'which minor?' The strength is like that for an overcall, varying a little with the vulnerability.

Negative double. (See page 129.) Nearly all tournament players employ a double of an overcall (for example, one spade-two clubs-double) for takeout, not penalties. How high this should apply needs agreement.

New minor forcing. If the opener's second bid is one notrump many tournament players agree that the cheaper unbid minor suit should be an artificial waiting move (one club-one heart; one notrump-two diamonds, for example).

Responsive double. When partner has overcalled or doubled and third hand has raised (one diamond-one spade-two diamonds, for example), a double can be for takeout by partnership agreement.

Roman Keycard Blackwood. Blackwood with special responses, counting the king of the trump suit as an ace, or keycard. Five clubs shows zero or three keycards, five diamonds one or four. To show two you bid five hearts (denying the queen of trumps) or five spades (promising that card).

SOS redouble. When a low-level contract is doubled for penalties, a redouble is a request that partner try something else.

Splinter. An unusual jump, skipping two levels, such as:

Opener	Responder		Opener	Responder
1♡	4♣		1♡	1♠
			4◇	

Shows slam interest, a good fit for partner (usually four cards) and at most one card in the suit bid.

Partners must agree whether this applies to direct jumps in a major suit (one club-three spades, or one spade-four hearts).

Strong club. Various systems using one club for all or nearly all strong hands. Other one-bids show minimum openings, with 11-15 or 11-16 high-card points. **Precision** is the most popular of these methods.

Strong raise. If partner opens, say, one spade, the responder may have a problem if he has good support and values for an opening bid.

The traditionalist can bid three spades, a forcing jump, but has problems with a hand worth about 11 points.

The modern player bids three spades with the 11-point hand but has a problem with 13-15. There are several possibilities: (a) with plenty of assets, but not more than 10 high-card points, bid four spades; (b) with a singleton or a void, use a splinter (see above); (c) by partnership agreement bid three notrump, giving up the standard meaning of 16-18 points and a balanced hand; (d) by partnership agreement bid two notrump (see *Jacoby Two Notrump* above); (e) failing these, bid a new suit and then jump to game in the opener's suit.

Transfer. (See page 152.) Special responses to one notrump and two notrump: diamonds shows heart length; hearts shows spade length; spades shows, usually, length in the minor suits. This is usually called Jacoby Transfer. A jump to the four-level ('Texas transfer') can be used similarly.

Two-way Stayman. A two-diamond response to one notrump can be used simply to ask for a major suit and guarantee game. Two clubs is still Stayman, but suggests a hand unable to guarantee game. This is an alternative to using transfers.

Unusual notrump. (See page 88.) An overcall of two notrump (two notrump over one heart, for example) shows a two-suiter, with at least five cards in each of the low-ranking unbid suits. The strength is like that for a normal overcall, allowing for vulnerability.

At the start of this book we skipped over the subject of scoring. The beginner can go a long way without knowing the details but now we must provide them. A difficulty is that the scoring changes slightly according to the form of bridge being played. Traditionally, the popular form of the game, as devised by Harold Vanderbilt in 1925, is **rubber bridge.** That has been dying out in North America, though not in other parts of the world. The replacement is **four-deal bridge,** also called **Chicago,** and this is now the normal game in North American clubs and homes.

FOUR-DEAL SCORING

1. Tricks bid and made count toward game at this rate:

Each trick in clubs and diamonds	20 points
Each trick in hearts and spades	30 points
In notrump, first trick	40 points
In notrump, subsequent tricks	30 points

   One hundred points earned in this way scores a game, which may be done in one, two, or conceivably more bites. Overtricks (made but not bid) count too, but not toward game.

2. Vulnerability is fixed: first deal, nobody vulnerable; second and third deals, dealer vulnerable; fourth deal, both sides vulnerable.

3. Bonuses (these do not count toward game) are scored on this basis:

Non-vulnerable game	300 points
Vulnerable game	500
Partscore on fourth deal	100

Small slam not vulnerable	500
Small slam vulnerable	750
Grand slam not vulnerable	1000
Grand slam vulnerable	1500
Honors: 4 of top 5 trumps in one hand	100
Honors: all 5 top trumps, or 4 aces at notrump, in one hand	150
For making a doubled contract	50
For making a redoubled contract	100

4. Doubled contracts if made score double the normal trick points, and redoubled contracts four times the normal points. So making two spades doubled or one spade redoubled (scoring 120 in each case) earns a game.

5. Defeated contracts normally suffer penalties on this scale: not vulnerable, 50 points each; vulnerable, 100 points each.

6. Defeated contracts suffer more when doubled: not vulnerable, first trick 100 points, second and third tricks 200 points, and later tricks 300 each; vulnerable, first trick 200 points and later tricks, 300 each (these penalties are exactly doubled again for redoubled contracts).

Nearly all this applies to all forms of bridge. But there is a divergence between duplicate and rubber bridge scoring.

DUPLICATE SCORING

(for tournaments and matches)

Each deal is scored separately, with vulnerability indicated on the duplicate board. Making a partscore always earns a bonus of 50 points. Honors do not count.

RUBBER BRIDGE SCORING

Vulnerability, instead of being arbitrary, is determined by the play. Scoring a game makes you vulnerable. Two games make a rubber, which earns a rubber bonus: 500 points if the opponents already have a game; 700 points if they do not.

LAWS

The Laws of Bridge are extensive and cover a wide variety of misdemeanors. A few of the most common (in simplified form) are:

1. *Insufficient bid* (for example, one heart-one club). You can make it legal by bidding two clubs without penalty. Any other action bars the offender's partner from further bidding and may require an opening lead penalty.

2. *Bid out of turn.* The bidding reverts to the correct player. If that is the right-hand opponent and he passes, the out-of-turn bid can be repeated without penalty; if he bids, the offender can repeat his bid, at a higher level if necessary, and his partner is barred for one round of bidding. In other situations the offender's partner is barred for the whole auction. There may be lead penalties.

3. *Lead out of turn* may be accepted by an opponent. If declarer's lead from the wrong hand is not accepted he must lead from the correct hand.

4. *Revoke* (discarding or ruffing by a player who could follow suit). If not corrected before the offending side has played to the next trick, the penalty is two tricks if the offending side won the revoke trick, otherwise one trick.

5. *Penalty card.* A spot card (below the ten) accidentally exposed must be played ahead of any other spot card of the same suit. Other exposed cards (honor cards, leads out of turn or attempted-revoke cards) are more serious. They must be played at the first opportunity, and there is a possible lead penalty if the offender's partner gains the lead.

6. *Claims.* If declarer claims the remaining tricks, or some of them, he must explain his line of play. Doubtful tricks go to the defense.

Any regular group of bridge players should keep a copy of the 1992 Laws handy to settle arguments. The Laws of Duplicate Bridge (revised in 1987) are slightly different.

BEHAVIOR

Some players make themselves unpopular at the bridge table by shouting and criticizing. Beyond the obvious requirements of good manners there are areas of propriety that are sometimes overlooked.

1. Do not comment on the bidding and play until the hand is over.

2. Bid in an even tone, avoiding indications of pleasure, displeasure, or doubt.

3. Do not draw any inference from partner's tone, hesitation, or behavior. (But you can draw inferences, at your own risk, from your opponents' behavior.)

Other points are listed in the Laws under 'Proprieties.'

WHAT ? NEXT

You have finished the book, and your bridge expertise is, I hope, much higher than when you began. What next?

PLAY

Reading, of course, is not enough. To increase your proficiency you must play as often as possible. If you have friends and neighbors who play you are in good shape. If not, look for the nearest bridge club. Most of them have programs for players at every level, novice to expert, and will be happy to see you.

To find a club in North America, write to: American Contract Bridge League, 2990 Airways Blvd., Memphis TN 38116. Ask for a Clubs Directory. It is free. This information, as well as all kinds of other bridge-related material, is also available online at **www.acbl.org**.

INSTRUCTION

If you find a club, its officials will usually be able to recommend a bridge teacher. If not, contact the American Contract Bridge League, as above, and ask for help.

If you find a teacher, you may want to verify his or her credentials. Ask him how long he has been a teacher, and what his playing rank is. A Life Master is probably competent.

OBSERVATION

Watching good players in action can be helpful. Ask your club officials to tell you when, and where, there is a major tournament (a Regional if possible) in your area. Ask a tournament director to point out a pair of experts who use standard bidding. (Avoid players using special systems.) Sit down and 'kibitz' quietly: do not ask questions or join in the conversation, since this is an unwelcome distraction to players who are trying to concentrate.

TOURNAMENTS

As well as kibitzing at a tournament, you may wish to play. There are nearly always novice games, and occasionally lectures for inexperienced players. Consider joining the American Contract Bridge League: for a small subscription you receive a big monthly magazine.

MORE READING

The game has an enormous literature. If you want a small library, try the following:

On bidding: *Commonsense Bidding*, by William Root, published by Crown.

On dummy-play: *Winning Declarer Play*, by Dorothy Hayden Truscott, published by Wilshire.

On defense: *Modern Bridge Defense* and *Advanced Bridge Defense*, both by Eddie Kantar, published by Master Point Press.

Advanced: any of the books of Hugh Kelsey or Michael Lawrence.

General: *Official Encyclopedia of Bridge*, published by ACBL.

These books, and many others, are available from major bridge-book distributors including the following:

Barclay Bridge Supplies,
3600 Chamberlain Lane, Louisville, KY 40241
1-800-274-2221 **www.baronbarclay.com**

Vince Oddy Bridge Supplies,
42 Stemmle Dr., Aurora, ON L4G 6N4
1-800-463-9815 **www.vinceoddy.com**

You may also get information about other bridge titles from the publisher of this book:

Master Point Press,
331 Douglas Avenue, Toronto, ON M5M 1H2
416-781-0351 **www.masterpointpress.com**

GLOSSARY

Asset A distributional value, which may vary with circumstances. Any long suit (more than four cards) or a singleton is an asset, and a void counts as 2 assets. Assets, which are equivalent to high-card points, disappear if no eight-card fit is found, double if there is a nine-card fit, and so on.

Attitude A defender's signal, encouraging the play of a suit (with a high card) or discouraging it (with a low card).

Auction The bidding period, before the play of the cards starts. As in a commercial auction, each bid must be higher than its predecessor.

Balanced An even hand distribution, typically four-three-three-three, four-four-three-two, or five-three-three-two. No singleton or void.

Balancing Reopening the bidding when the opponents have stopped at a low level. Advisable when they have found a fit, inadvisable against notrump.

Bid An announcement such as 'one club' (seven tricks with clubs as trumps), which may end the auction, and so determine the trump suit and target for the play. Often, however, a step toward such a final contract.

Bidding The auction period, preceding the play. After the dealer acts, it takes three consecutive passes, at any point, to end the bidding.

Blackwood Artificial use of a four notrump bid to ask partner how many aces he has. Responses are by steps: five clubs, none; five diamonds, one, and so forth. Raises of notrump (for example, one notrump-four notrump) are natural slam invitations, not Blackwood.

Block A suit situation in which it is not possible to take high-card tricks directly (for example, singleton king opposite ace-small). An entry in another suit is needed, and such problems should usually be tackled quickly.

Chicago The standard social four-deal game, which has largely replaced rubber bridge. See page 218.

Claim An announcement, usually by the declarer, that play can be terminated because the outcome is clear. The claimer may want all the remaining tricks, or some of them, or none of them. The opponents should verify that he is right.

Contract The final bid, anything from one club to seven notrump, perhaps doubled or redoubled, which determines the declarer's play target.

Count A defender's signal to show the number of cards in an opposing long suit, usually dummy's suit. A high card shows an even number, and a low card an odd number, aimed at helping partner to judge a possible hold-up play.

Declarer The player who controls his own hand and the dummy, attempting to fulfill the contract. If the contract is, for example, seven clubs, the first member of the partnership to bid clubs becomes the declarer.

Discard A card play made by a player who cannot follow suit and is unable (or unwilling) to trump. A discard cannot win a trick.

Distribution The pattern (or 'shape') of the suits in one hand, such as four-four-three-two or five-four-three-one, or the division of a suit around the table.

Double A bid that announces a desire to defeat an opposing contract and inflict a bigger penalty, but often used in a specialized way. (See *Lead-Directing Bid, Negative double, Responsive double* and *Takeout.*)

Doubleton A suit with exactly two cards.

Duck Conceding a trick that could be won, often with the intention of developing an extra trick or two in the suit.

Dummy Declarer's partner, who takes no part in the play, or his cards, which are face up on the table after the opening lead is made.

Duplicate Various forms of competitive bridge in which each deal is played at least twice and the results are compared.

Endplay See *Throw-in.*

Favorable vulnerability Being not vulnerable against vulnerable opponents, and therefore inclined to compete aggressively and perhaps save.

Finesse An attempt to take advantage of a favorable location of the opposing cards in a suit.

Fit The number of cards the partnership has in its most promising suit. Eight cards is acceptable, more is desirable.

Forcing A bid that tells partner to do something, and on no account to pass. It may be forcing for one round (one diamond-one spade) or game-forcing (one diamond-two notrump).

Four-deal See *Chicago.*

Game A contract that earns a big bonus (or in rubber bridge the prospect of one). Three notrump, four hearts, four spades, five clubs, five diamonds, or anything higher equal game.

Grand slam A bid of seven, contracting to make all the tricks in the hope of earning a big bonus — 1000 or 1500 according to vulnerability.

Hold-up A refusal to win a trick that could be won, usually in a suit in which an opponent is long and strong.

Honor An ace, king, queen, jack, or ten.

Jump A bid that skips at least one level (for example, one spade-three spades).

Lead The right (and duty) to play the first card to a trick. It belongs to the player who won the previous trick. (Except at the start: the opening lead is made by the player on declarer's left.)

Lead-directing bid Usually a double, aimed at helping partner to find the winning lead. A double of three notrump says: lead your suit, or my suit, or dummy's suit, in that order of preference. A double of an artificial bid shows length and strength in the suit. (See *Lightner* for doubles of slams).

Lightner A double of a slam to suggest an unusual lead. The doubler usually has a void suit and therefore wants a ruff, or he wants dummy's suit led.

Limit In general, any accurate, non-forcing descriptive bid. For example, the invitational jump raise (one spade-three spades) as distinct from the traditional forcing raise.

Major The high-ranking suits, spades and hearts.

Minor The low-ranking suits, diamonds and clubs.

Misfit Inability to find an eight-card or better trump fit.

Negative double A takeout double used when an opening bid has been overcalled.

Non-forcing Any natural action that does not require partner to bid.

Notrump A bid that suggests playing without a trump suit. Usually it is natural and describes a balanced hand.

Opening lead The first card played, by the player on declarer's left, on any deal.

Overcall The first bid, if something other than a double, made by the side that does not open the bidding.

Overruff Playing a higher trump than an opponent after another suit has been led.

Overtrick A trick taken when the contract has already been fulfilled (unimportant except in duplicate).

Partscore A contract below game, with a small value. In rubber bridge or Chicago, two (conceivably more) partscores can be combined to make a game.

Pass A negative announcement, showing no immediate desire to take part in the auction.

Pass-out (or throw-in) Four passes at the start of the auction, ending the proceedings. There is no play and no score for either side.

Penalty   Points received by a partnership that defeats an opposing contract, or a double aimed at increasing these points.

Phantom   An unwise save, losing points when the opponents would have been defeated.

Play   The period following the auction. Each player contributes a card to each trick, in clockwise order, producing thirteen tricks.

Point   Either a scoring point (see page 218) or a high-card point on the 4-3-2-1 scale (see page 13).

Preempt (or preemptive bid)   A weak opening suit bid of two diamonds or higher based on a long suit.

Preference   Returning to partner's first suit. Unless made with a jump, this is a weak action showing two- or three-card support. Do it with equal length, because partner's first suit is often longer.

Rebid   The second bid by any player.

Redouble   In theory, an attempt to increase the stakes again when an opponent has doubled for penalties. In practice, usually a way of showing strength when an opponent has made a takeout double or of sending an SOS message after a low-level penalty double.

Restricted choice   A principle of play that recommends a finesse when a possibility of one develops unexpectedly. Suppose that you have A-5-4-2 facing K-10-7-6-3 in dummy. If the ace collects the queen or jack from your right-hand opponent, finesse the ten.

Reverse   A rebid by opener showing a second suit and a strong hand, about 18 points. It is always a bid that makes it impossible to return to the first suit at the two-level (for example, one club-one spade; two hearts).

Revoke   Failure to follow suit when legally obliged to do so. The penalty is one or two tricks according to circumstances.

Ruff   To trump a trick, or the play of a trump when another suit has been led.

Save or Sacrifice   A bid made (usually at favorable vulnerability) with no expectation of success. The hope is to lose less than the value of the opposing contract, or perhaps push the opponents to an unsafe contract.

Side suit   A secondary suit (not trumps), usually of four cards.

Singleton   A suit with exactly one card.

Skip   A jump bid, bypassing one or more levels.

Slam   A contract of six or seven, requiring twelve or thirteen tricks to be made, in the hope of a large bonus.

Small slam   A contract of six, earning a bonus of 500 or 750 according to vulnerability.

Spot card   Any small card below the ten.

Squeeze   A play that takes advantage of an opponent's inability to guard two suits at once.

Stayman   An artificial bid in response to notrump (one notrump-two clubs, or two notrump-three clubs), asking the opener to bid a four-card (or five-card) major suit. Lacking one, he bids diamonds.

Stopper or guard   A holding such as an ace, a king doubleton, or a queen tripleton, which is likely to prevent the opponents taking a string of tricks in a notrump contract.

Suit   Clubs, diamonds, hearts or spades.

Suit preference   A defender's signal pointing to another suit, a low card for a low-ranking suit and a high card for a high-ranking suit. Only applies if other signals (attitude or count) clearly do not.

Takeout   A double asking partner to select a suit (see page 97).

Throw-in   A play to give an opponent the lead when it will be to your advantage (see also *Pass-out*).

Transfer bid   An artificial response to one or two notrump, showing length in the next-higher suit.

Trick   Four cards, one from each player, played in clockwise sequence. The highest trump wins if there is one, otherwise the highest card of the suit led wins.

Tripleton   A suit with exactly three cards.

Trump   A card of the suit named in the contract, or to play such a card, thus winning the trick unless a higher trump is played.

Unblock   A play to resolve a block. For example, if your partner leads a queen and you have a doubleton king you should usually play the king to get out of his way.

Undertrick   Each trick by which the declarer fails in his contract.

Unfavorable   Being vulnerable against non-vulnerable opponents. A bad time to contest the bidding aggressively.

Void   A suit in which no cards are held.

Vulnerable   The state of having a game. Penalties and bonuses are bigger.

x   Used in bridge literature to represent any small card below the ten.

Yarborough   A hand with no card above a nine. Loosely, any very weak hand.

INDEX